How To: Start a Home Staging Business with $2500 and THRIVE!

By: Amy Latawiec
Founder of Acute Designer, LLC
Home Staging and Interior Design

Copyright © 2025

All Rights Reserved

ISBN:

Dedication

I dedicate this book to all those girl bosses out there trying to make a difference in this world and working your butt off to make something of yourself. Keep going, keep pushing, keep supporting each other. We only have one life, let's make it the best we can!

Acknowledgement

This book could not have been completed without the support of my amazing family and friends. So thankful for my dedicated husband, Tristan, for giving me support and time to write this for you. Thank you for all the meals you cooked and all the times you helped out with Hailey. Love you sweet man. Thank you to my amazing daughter, Hailey, for allowing me to step away from watching her play sports and write many nights in the luxury of the front seat of my car in the parking lot at her practices. I was always there in spirit, my Hailey bug. Thank you to my loving mother, Marilyn, for many phone calls working through the blocks and hardships getting this completed. I truly appreciate your support mom! Thank you to my brothers Jon, Brad, and Ethan for all your encouragement and excitement to keep me going on this journey. Thank you to my amazing grandparents, Samuel aka Poppie and Deborah, for all your wisdom, love, and support for pushing me to start this book and share my journey with the world. A special thank you to Deborah for taking the time to proofread and edit this book for me. I am honored you would help me complete this part of the writing process. I am just so grateful for everyone else who has supported me and knew I could finish this. It was a lot of long nights and days getting this done and my hope is that I can give back and help support others on their entrepreneurial journey and bring their dreams to fruition. Cheers y'all!

Table of Contents

Dedication ii

Acknowledgement iii

About the Author 1

Introduction 2

Chapter 1: What the Heck is Home Staging? 7

Chapter 2: Research, Research, Research, Then Research Some More. 14

Chapter 3: First Things First. 36

Chapter 4: Make An Appearance Online. 53

Chapter 5: Market the Hell Out of Yourself. 64

Chapter 6: First Staging Project Requested. What Do I Do???!!! 80

Chapter 7: Get Ready, Get Set, GOALS! 103

Chapter 8: Maintain and Thrive. 114

About the Author

Amy Latawiec earned her bachelor's degree in interior design from Texas Tech University in Lubbock, Texas in 2006. Amy established her design career at several companies in Whidbey Island, Washington and Charleston, South Carolina. She then decided to follow her other passion, teaching, and received her Master's degree in Art of Teaching at College of Charleston in Charleston, South Carolina in 2014. After experiencing great accomplishments in her education career, Amy then decided to jump back into her first love and passion of design here in Denver, Colorado and founded Acute Designer, LLC. As an interior designer and home stager, Latawiec's main focus is serving the client to the best of her ability. Amy works on projects of all sizes, from complete design services to simply helping clients choose the perfect paint colors for their home. Interior design and home staging is not just a job for Amy – it's a passion. She enjoys building relationships with all kinds of clients, and enjoys the variety of experiences a design career provides. She also uses her talents to educate the public about what interior design and home staging involves and how clients can continue to love their space. The continued relationship and impact of the finished design with each client is very rewarding to Amy.

Introduction

Do you ever find yourself styling or decorating your home all the time, even between the seasons? Do you enjoy helping family and friends restyle their spaces? When going to department stores, do you make a b-line straight to the home section? Do you ever catch yourself binge watching design shows all weekend? Do you ever wonder how you can make design or decorating more than a hobby? Do you have $2,500 sitting in an account or rainy-day fund? If you do any of these things and have the cash, you might be in the right place! I am here to help you begin a new era in your life and get you started on a journey of creating the business of your dreams!

I began my decorating and design career back when I was a teenager. I'm sure it drove my mother crazy that every weekend I would move furniture and decor around in my room and all around the house. As a teen, I only wished for home decor for birthday gifts and presents from my family members (and maybe a lot of shoes too). I loved it. I was passionate about it all. Growing up, I was so blessed that one of my best friends' mothers was an interior designer and gave me the perfect inspiration I needed for college and my future. She also pushed me in a direction to try out an internship in high school and work for a local designer to get even more experience in the field. I was hooked. So, my senior year in high school, I applied to Texas Tech University, which was known to have a great design program. I was then accepted into the school in the Interior Design program in 2002 and graduated four years later with my Bachelors in Interior Design and a minor in Architecture.

    I always had a passion for design and was eager to start a business one day to help serve others. I just didn't know what type of design business, yet. Most of all, I was scared to take the leap. It took 11 years and a lot of different types of design jobs in numerous cities to find my passion. Things always work out the way they are supposed to and I am so glad I jumped when the opportunity arose. Timing couldn't have been better, I was deciding whether or not to move to a new state for a fresh start and one of my brothers, Jon, called me up about a chance to work with him on his new builds as his designer and stager in the Denver metro area. I give mad props to my brother, Jon (and still do). Jon took a chance on me and helped me start the business of my dreams. He showed me the way and put me on a path that I had never known existed, Home Staging. I moved from South Carolina to Colorado and within the first week of the move in June of 2017, I founded and created Acute Designer Home Staging and Interior Design and have been nonstop since.

The Learning Experience

Even though I run a successful business now, there have been many ups and downs and struggles along the way. When I started the company, I was a new entrepreneur with absolutely no experience and just moved to a new city! What the hell was I thinking?! I did not take any business courses during my college career so I had no idea where to start. I did have a little bit of help from my brother and my very first business partner, Grace, to get the website and social media active, but I still had so much to learn!!

The first year of the business was slow and I used this time to go through a local business course with the city. So glad I found that resource because the class helped me understand the basic in's and out's of the business industry and how to make sure my business would survive. It helped me understand how important finding my "niche" was in the business world and how to truly focus on the right clients. If you have the time, check out your city resources. This would be an amazing way to help shape and mold the business you want for yourself and do it before you get started! I went at this ass backwards, but I got it done!

The biggest struggle during the beginning of the business was cash flow. So thankful I had savings in the bank and had extra cash from just selling my South Carolina home, but I learned very quickly that I should have not "quit my day job" just yet. I'm so grateful that my second business partner, Victoria (still my ride or die sidekick), was able to also go without taking a paycheck from the business during this time too. This gave us a full year to gain momentum, add to our inventory of furniture, pay bills, and start our nest egg. During this year, I had to take on a full-time job to pay my personal bills once all my savings ran out. It was a tough year working 7 days a week and 12-16 hour days. I missed a lot of my kiddo's sports and activities, and lost time with my family. But it was a short sacrifice that my family and I made in order to have the dream job now, along with extra time with my family too. Overall, it takes time setting up a business, growing a business, maintaining a business, purchasing resources to help fulfill your business services, and most importantly actually seeing revenue in your pocket from the business. So, the learning experience here is that before you start any new business adventure, make sure you have at least 9-12 months of monthly savings in the bank or continue to work your current job and start the new biz as a side hustle. Now, if I haven't scared you off yet, keep reading! Why am I sharing all this with you? Because I want to help you succeed in the beginning and not run into major problems like the ones that I experienced. I plan to provide you with a step-by-step plan to get your business going using a lot of creativity and with a small amount of cash in your pocket. That shouldn't be hard for you since you love design and decorating! That IS creativity!

My goal for this book is to help guide you through the process of starting your own home staging business as well as having a smart strategy to do it. I want to help you be successful, and get your business started with only $2500! No going into debt, no help from investors or loans, just sweat equity. It can be done. If you have the drive, the passion, the willingness to be creative, the eagerness to get your hands dirty, the support from family and friends, then go for it! I am so glad I stuck it out especially through the hard times, because having this business is so fulfilling. I have made some amazing friendships and created long lasting relationships. I have helped thousands of clients and made a difference in their lives. That is why I love what I do, and I want you to love it too!

Chapter 1: What the Heck is Home Staging?

Back to the basics. So, what is Home Staging, you ask? Home Staging is a service provided to sellers, real estate agents, builders, or flippers. These clients request that the home is prepped and "staged" in order to sell on the real estate market. When a home is staged, the ultimate goal is to make as many buyers as possible see the amazing potential of the home and buy it. What does that mean? Home staging shows off the best parts of the home so buyers can visualize themselves living there without hesitation. Staging also helps provide a special awareness of what size furniture can actually fit in the space. According to data from the Real Estate Staging Association (RESA) it is known that 75% of sellers saw a ROI or Return of Investment of 5-15% over asking price when using staging to sell their home. This is great when staging costs are usually up to 1% of the sale price of the home! This makes all clients a bit happier too knowing our services truly can make a huge difference in the sale of the home!

There are several ways you can stage a home. Vacant staging, partial staging, and occupied staging. I will break these down individually so you can decide what could work best for your business model and plan.

Vacant Staging

Vacant staging occurs when the sellers move out of the home or the builder/flipper has finished the work and the home is completely empty of furnishings. Furniture, accessories, art, rugs, lamps, linens, towels, etc. are brought in to be staged/set up in the most desirable rooms of the home to entice the buyers and help them visualize how they could set up the spaces themselves. With our business, on average, we stage the living room, dining room, primary bedroom, and add accessories in the kitchen and baths. If a home has multiple living spaces and dining spaces, we tend to stage those areas as well to show off the large floorplan of the home. Some sellers or realtors we work with will request that we stage every room in the home. Most of the time, the client trusts our opinion of what areas to stage but be sure to always ask what they want staged, never assume. **Side note: The most important thing to do is communicate with your client and find out what their expectations are with the project as well as understand their budget.

There are two major types of vacant staging: luxury and standard/basic. Luxury staging typically will showcase higher end furniture pieces, art, rug, accessories, etc. Clients will also pay a premium for the staging costs because higher end homes require upscale furniture to match the level of the home. The market value/cost of living in your area is your best determination of where luxury staging could start. For instance, in our market, we consider staging homes with luxury furniture above $2 Million give or take. Now that does not mean you couldn't always use luxury/high end furniture as your main staging whether the home is $150,000 or $6 Million. That is up to your marketing and business model. But, always check your area and research your competition to see how they structure their staging plans and costs! We will chat more about researching later in the book!

Standard/basic staging will cover the rest of the market. This could be as little as a tiny studio apartment to a five/six bedroom home. With basic staging, you still want to use decent furniture pieces and keep up with the current trends. What defines the difference between luxury and standard is how you market your staging business. We will discuss marketing strategies later in the book.

Above: Before and after photos of a vacant stage

Partial Staging

Partial staging can mean multiple things. Sometimes sellers have already moved out of their home, however, they weren't able to take all the furniture with them or they would like to leave some items to keep staging costs lower. We run into many different scenarios but essentially in this case, we need to add items from our inventory with the sellers' current furniture already in the home. Other situations with partial staging can include bringing in some furniture or accessories into an occupied home to help make the home feel more aesthetically pleasing. This is when sellers are living in the home while it is listed on the market. **Side note: This can get a little dicey. Over the years, we have put in place that we will not partially stage an occupied home with pets and young kids. Too much inventory has been damaged!! Again, this is where your business strategy and marketing can be unique to you!

With partial staging, the costs are typically lower than a normal stage because you are not bringing in as many items. However, be sure to outweigh the labor costs of your time to prep and stage along with the costs of the moving itself. Sometimes, we ended up charging a full stage package because we brought in just as much furniture as we would for a simple vacant staging package. Always calculate the costs before giving the client a quick answer on the cost of the project. Your time is valuable and not free!! I can't tell you enough how important it is to also take the time before the business is off the ground to research the competition and see what they offer and how they offer it. More on this in another section!

Occupied Staging Consults/Reports

If you truly love making a difference in people's lives, this side of the business is where it's at. In our line of business, we are not just stagers. We are therapists, advisors, cheerleaders, and teachers. Over the years, I have helped thousands of clients "rip off the band-aids" and start the moving process, gain knowledge in home design, understand the beauty of simplifying, learn how to let go of the "stuff", be advocates for themselves, and so much more. When we show up for an occupied staging consultation, the sellers are graciously letting us into their personal/intimate lives to see how they live and have lived for sometimes 30 years in the same home. It takes a lot of empathy from us to express that we are there to help support them. Moving is a very stressful time for most. So, when I personally can provide assistance and ease their stress, I feel I have done my job.

An occupied staging consultation usually consists of meeting the clients at the home and walking through each space while providing feedback on how they can present the room in the best possible light. This could consist of removing larger pieces of furniture. I might also suggest removing personal pictures and art that might be too dramatic for some tastes. It might include rearranging furniture in the space or bringing a chair from one room to another. My favorite part is getting creative with what the sellers currently have. It's like a puzzle that I have to put together. The most important thing when providing feedback is to make sure the room feels spacious and neutral to all types of buyers. The consults usually last around 45 minutes to an hour depending on the size of the home.

While I walk through the home, I take pictures of the spaces for reference (always ask first to take pictures and explain to the clients why you are taking them so they feel at ease). I found over the years that taking notes is too much work and time. When I take photos, I can also revisit them later when writing up a report and still feel like I am there at the house so I do not forget what we spoke about. With all this said, our business model includes a written report with the consultant. This is where we write up a report or checklist for the sellers of what we discussed during the consultation. This is very helpful because the clients can refer back to the report on what needs to be adjusted. I try my best to not over complicate the report and keep it straight forward. Create a template that you can use every time, so you are not reinventing the wheel! Sometimes, I am asked to physically help move some things around and adjust art, accessories, etc. I do make sure I know in advance if my help is needed in this way so I can plan and charge accordingly. Sometimes, this can take a few hours so be sure to understand what the clients need before making the trek out to the home! If they also want a report after the consultation, then I charge for the additional hour/s I am there. **Side note: I will not move large furniture by myself. This is a whole different ball game. If the sellers can't move the furniture, then I come up with a different solution for them.

After the consultation and report, I offer my services via text or email. I have some clients who want reassurance or just confirmation they did a good job so I ask them to send photos via text. I found I respond much faster this way. But yes, an occupied staging consult is typically a one and done visit at the home. If I need to go back, then I do charge for my time. Again, your time is valuable!!

Now that you have a knowledge of what Home Staging can consist of, want to give it a go? Want to take the leap and create your dream job too? Let's jump in!

Chapter 2: Research, Research, Research, Then Research Some More.

I'm so glad I love to research things because that was my saving grace in the beginning. Since I was a newbie at all this, I wanted to gain confidence and knowledge of the industry and know what I was up against. I spent hours looking into other staging companies in the area and learning what they offered and how they marketed themselves online. I also researched furniture rental companies as well as furniture costs from local stores and online marketplaces to get a sense of what the overall price tag might be to stage a whole house. My research did not stop there. Other things I looked into were types of business websites out there, how and where to store my inventory, and so much more. Now, I know some of you are probably thinking, "I just want to jump in and go!" You can certainly do that, but mistakes will happen, and you could be unprepared at the worst times while trying to create a good, established business. I will tell you though, some of these items below do not always need to be researched up front. I start the research list with the most important items and work my way down to the topics that should be looked into but can certainly wait until after the business gets going. With that said, I know that my due diligence and time spent researching in the beginning has kept my business successful and running smoothly. Follow along. I will break it down in a simple way of what things to look into so you are empowered with as much knowledge as you can get into your brain. This will help prepare you and start your glorious path to creating your business!

Local Staging Companies

This type of research is crucial so you can be sure you are not pricing yourself out of the market. It also helps to see what types of companies are out there and decide what direction you want your business to go. Luxury? Affordable? Partial? You decide. To start the process, your best friend will be Google. I started the search by typing in "Home Staging Denver CO" because I wanted to know what companies were in my local area. This type of search will get you in the ballpark of who is out there and see those bigger companies that are paying for the status to show up first on the search engine. Start here with the larger companies, but once you get more comfortable, start digging in further to see some of the little guys on the lower part of the list (like me!). I don't pay SEO companies a monthly fee to bring me to the top of the list. This helps save money. But that is for another section.

There are several things to look for when searching through websites, instagram pages, tiktok, etc.

- **Services Offered and Prices**: Focus on the descriptions of services and how the companies price them out. Some companies will provide their starting out prices to give you a baseline. These prices can depend on square footage, design style, or premium (luxury) inventory. Some companies will make you click on a link to ask for a consult so they can gain your info to add you as a possible client. This is smart for them so they obtain your info but hard for you to get an idea of their pricing. That's when you pick up the phone and pretend to be a client to get some pricing from them. (Cold calling is not fun but crucial). Along with pricing, also ask how their process goes from beginning to end. For example, does their price include delivery, staging the property, and removing it? How many rooms will they stage? How long does the staging cost cover? Can you extend it if the house doesn't sell right away and how much does it cost? If I am living in the house during the sale of the home, can my dog stay with me? What if my house sells before the end of the month or staging lease, do I get my money back if the furniture is removed early? How far out of town will you stage? I did this to many companies so I could understand the market pricing and get an idea of how the companies presented themselves over the phone. I would call multiple places and ask a few questions per place. It really helped me pull my business model together. Don't feel bad about this part because I know over the years that some people did the very same thing to me too. It's part of the business and I would just play along and be kind. **Side note: Use this time to get an idea of how you would charge for a stage. This will be important later when I discuss the ins and outs of costing out a job, etc.

- **Website Layout:** After taking the time to see what services are offered, I took a step back and analyzed their websites. I looked at how many tabs/pages they had and what each tab represented. For example, some tabs/pages were labeled "Home Staging Services" or "About Us", or "Portfolio". I scrolled through their website to see how easy or hard it was to navigate through. I paid attention to whose site I liked best and why. I made lots of notes and took screen shots of the layouts I liked. This will help you when you get ready to create your own website.

- **Portfolio/Recent Projects/Photos:** I took even more time going through their photos of their work. This is super helpful when you might not feel as confident in the design/decorating aspect. You have guidelines with their work. Notice what you like and what you don't like. Pay attention to how they layout the furniture according to the room size and orientation. How are they staging around a fireplace or how do they stage with an open concept layout? See how they are putting rooms together with all their accessories. Check out the artwork used and the bedding. All these little details can give you inspiration when you are ready to start staging!

- **Social Media:** One of the last things I researched on the companies was their social media presence. I wanted to understand how they were showing up and on what platforms. I did not spend too much time here in the beginning because I always seem to get sucked up into the endless scrolling. But we will get to social media in a later section.

Furniture and Accessory Costs

Once you have an idea on how you want to model your business, then start the research on how much the actual furniture will cost you. Again, if you want to go luxury, then you must have nicer end furniture pieces and accessories. This can get quite pricey in the beginning and if you want to start this business with $2500 and thrive, I highly suggest focusing on the basic staging to start. If you are in a big city, you should have plenty of resources to check out online or in person. If you are in a smaller town, it might be best to check out the local stores in person to see the deals. I will tell you, I purchase a lot online and have it shipped to my home. Then I break out the champagne and have a building party on the weekends with my husband and my daughter. It's great. I love it. They love it. My trash guys love it. Any who, jot down the costs of the average sofa price, accent chair, coffee table, etc. It helps if you create a list of items in each space that you would typically need to stage. Once you get an idea, then figure out the total cost so you can have an understanding of the cost difference between what you are charging the client vs. what you are spending.

See an example list below of a minimum basic vacant stage of what items will potentially be needed per room.

- **Living Room**: sofa, loveseat or two chairs, coffee table, two end tables, console table or sofa table (I use these to act as tv stand/entertainment pieces-not as bulky and easier to store when not in use), rug, artwork (typically 2-3 depending on size of room), two table lamps, throw pillows, accessories for the tables

- **Dining Room**: dining table, 4-6 chairs, rug, console table or sofa table, artwork (1-2 pieces), accessories for the tables

- **Bedroom**: typically a queen bed with base frame for an average size room, possible headboard (or you can use taller pillows on the bed or lower artwork), bed linens, 2 nightstands, console table or accent chair or both depending on the size of the room, artwork (1-2 pieces), table lamps for nightstands, accessories for tables

- **Home Office**: a simple desk and desk chair, accent chair or chairs, simple bookcase or console table, rug, artwork (1-2 pieces), accessories

- **Kitchen**: kitchen accessories for the counters, possible barstools if there is an island, possible runner for the floor

- **Bathrooms:** towels, artwork (1 piece), accessories for the counter and sometimes around the tub area

Now, this seems like a ton of stuff. It is but, when I first started out, I had a few tricks up my sleeve. My business partner and I "shopped" our own houses in the beginning so we could keep costs down until we could eventually buy everything new. We also used consignment shops and online marketplaces that are selling used "like new" pieces. These tricks truly saved a lot so we could make these first stages look amazing and not bare and empty.

However, it is still so important to make these lists so you can really see the bottom-line number of what a stage can cost you. Never assume, always take the time to cost it out or you will never get ahead. It is so easy to start buying things (because that can be the fun part and we all know how Target can suck you in) and then all of a sudden your cost of inventory is twice what you are charging a client. Just an FYI, our focus on the first several stages was to try to break even. The beauty of this is, once you get back the staging items, they go to another home and the future stages become less and less costly over time. Then you finally start to see more revenue in your pocket.

Moving Companies/Storage Units

If you do not have a truck and trailer already or a place to store the inventory, this section is for you. When I started out, my garage was my storage unit for our inventory. This saved a lot of money in the beginning. However, we had no trailers or trucks. Both my business partner and I drove lovely SUV's instead (these come in handy my friends-my car is never empty of accessories and storage bins). So, I had to quickly research my local area to see how I could get the furniture to and from my place. I researched several types of moving companies. One company that I looked into would give me a 3 hour window of when they would show up with their truck and then have two guys move the stuff from our garage into the staged home. We tried this for a while and did not like their process so we moved on. The cost for this ranged between $400-$500 each move. To keep the cost down, I then looked into moving the furniture ourselves too.

(If you are young and motivated, go for it, but let me tell you, I am 40 and some days feel 80 with my back after 7 years of moving furniture here and there. Make it make sense for you). Then we looked into the storage companies who offer rental trucks/moving vans to rent for the day. Some of them even offer extra labor, two movers would show up where we needed them to start, load the truck, and then meet you at the destination. Take the time to see which ones are of value for you and your business. Overall, moving expenses in this scenario could cost you up to $250. Definitely saves money. We ended up eventually needing more space to store items, and one of the moving companies that we rented trucks from gave us a free month of rental on a storage unit. Saving money, my favorite!

Big questions to ask when calling around:

- What are the day fees for truck rentals?

- What are the mileage fees?

- What are the available storage units and sizes?

- Are they climate controlled?

- Can I rent the storage units month to month or do you have a discount for `renting them for 6 months to a year at a time?

- Do you offer services to hire out labor/help?

- What is the cost of extra labor if needed?

**Side note: Furniture likes climate controlled spaces. If you are in a hot, humid climate and put wood furniture in a non climate controlled unit, you will be very disappointed. On the other extreme, if you are in a dry, cold area, furniture will hate that too without the climate control. Cheaper is not always better in this situation!

Business Structures/Articles of Organization/Operating Agreements

This might not seem like a fun research topic but it is critical to know what type of business you want to set up. This will also be important for when you actually register your business with the state and start the tax process. If you feel as if you want experienced advice, talk with a local accountant. They will charge an hourly rate of $200-250 for their time. If you want to keep it free and keep under $2500 to start up the business, there is an excellent resource for all of us small business owners to use!

The Small Business Administration has an amazing website, www.sba.gov with free advice and information on how to set up a business and where to go from there. The "Business Guide" has everything! You can find a whole section on choosing a business structure from LLC to Corp. The website breaks down what each type of structure looks like. LLC is a great way to go for a small business. It is simple and less expensive to start. Also, if you have minimal people working for you, it makes taxes easy come the end of the year.

There are two documents that you will need to create if you set up an LLC: an Articles of Organization and an Operating Agreement. Articles of Organization declares your intent to create an LLC in whatever state you chose to register and operate your business. An Operating Agreement gives the identity of the member(s), scope of the business, function of the business, and limitations. Banks will often ask for the document when you open up a checking account so they have understanding of your business as well. You can find both of these as free templates online. The SBA website also has great info on both documents. This is a great time to research both docs and find a template you like best.

There are several types of LLC options you could choose from for your business. Single-Member LLC, Partnership, or Multi-Member LLC. Check out the types below.

- **Single-Member LLC**

    If you decide to open up the business by yourself, I highly suggest creating a single-member LLC. This type of business allows you to be a separate entity from yourself. It protects your personal assets from the company's debts and obligations. You are able to hire employees and open up a business account. The opposite of this type of business is a Sole Proprietorship which keeps you liable for the business debts, losses, and obligations. It is best to keep you and your business separate so I suggest Single-Member LLC over Sole Proprietorship!

    Like I mentioned before, it is essential to create an operating agreement for your business. An operating agreement allows you to define and prove your separation. It can also increase your credibility with investors and bankers. You will need to have an operating agreement to open up a banking account so it is definitely important to create this. The agreement also allows you to create rules for your business as well as define where your liabilities and assets go if the LLC needs to be dissolved. These are pretty easy to set up and you can easily find free templates online!

- **Partnership**

    Another type of LLC is a partnership. This is when you decide to go into business with a friend or family member. Partnerships are great but it is so important to have a straight forward contract or agreement with your partner just in case things change over time.

    If you decide to go into business with a partner, research partnership agreements online. There are several free versions/templates available on the web. These types of agreements are great to break down the in's and out's of how you will run the partnership in a business like manner. If someone needs to remove themselves from the partnership, the agreement will explain how that will take place. It can also describe contributions and disbursements to each partner. The agreement can also explain how the company will be dissolved if necessary. Having a partnership agreement also avoids costly legal proceedings and can end on your terms. If you do not have an agreement in place and the business needs to dissolve, you will have to close your business on the states' partnership terms and laws.

- **LLC with more than two members**

    If you have several folks that will be creating this business together, then look into forming an LLC with multiple members. In this case, definitely set up an operating agreement to discuss the nuts and bolts of your business. This agreement should be written between the members of your business to describe your managing structure, disbursements, contributions, etc. It also allows you to set up the registered agent who will be the main contact for the business. Having an agreement will prevent disputes among members and define members' roles. This will clarify so much and not create confusion among the members.

Secretary of State-Filing/Creation of Business/IRS

Once you have done your research and made the decision of what structure of business you will run, it is now time to research the Secretary of State website for the state you live in and will conduct the business. You will find out how to create/register the business and file the necessary paperwork for the state on this website. Each state is different in how to file and their price structures can vary state to state but use this time to nail down what you need. This is an important research step because it is necessary to go through the Secretary of State to set up the business so the state knows who you are. This will allow you to add your business name and info to the state's website so no one else can take your business name, when you are ready to register and begin the business. I will guide you through how to register later but it is important to go through this website and gain familiarity with it so you are comfortable using it. I have to go on this website at least once a year to file the annual report to keep a "good standing" with the state so I added this website as a favorite so I can always find it quickly on my computer.

Also use this time also to research how to apply for your Tax ID number. This will be done with the IRS and created through their website, www.irs.gov. You will need this as soon as you register your business with the state in order to file taxes, get a checking account, etc. The SBA website gives a little more information about this too but it is super easy to register through the IRS. I give step by step instructions later in the book on this.

Business Plans/Mission Statements

Now, I do know several business owners who have never written out a business plan, but this is an important step if you ever need investors or financing for your business. The plan also helps shape your values, your marketing, your future model of the business, projections of the business, and how you plan to control the business. I highly recommend taking time to research already completed business plans by other people so you can see what info is included. Don't reinvent the wheel, there are lots of free templates out there online as well as different types of plans (traditional or lean startup).

- **Traditional Business Plan:** traditional plans are very detail-oriented and are required for most traditional sources of financing.

- **Lean Startup Business Plan:** these plans are quick to write up and include the key elements of your business. This is a great way to start you in a forward direction but most investors will need more info to help finance you if needed.

Again, use the SBA website. They have business plan templates on their site but you can find quite a few others just by searching the web. If you just don't see the need to create a business plan, I get it. There are tons of self made millionaires and billionaires who have never written one. I mean I technically have never needed one at all because I have never needed start-up loans or investments from others. BUT, I highly suggest researching business plans and eventually creating one for your company.

One thing to definitely create for your business is a mission statement.

- **Mission Statement:** a mission statement is a brief explanation of a business' ideas, goals, objectives, and how they will be achieved.

Mission statements are the bones of the business that provide structure, your values for the business, and what you want the business to become and how. Mission statements are also the heart and soul of the business too. They are the "Why" you want to do this in the first place, the passion, the integrity, the service to others. They are short and sweet but give your future clients a true understanding of who you are.

If you have no desire to write a business plan, at least look into mission statements and how they are structured so you can start thinking about your future business. I highly encourage you to create a mission statement for your business. It will help you market your business and let future clients know your intentions. You also want to include your mission statement on your business website or marketing materials so it is definitely important to research templates and other mission statements in order to have the confidence to create your own.

Website Creator/Templates/Domain

If you want to be recognized and found, you must have a website. Nowadays, more and more clients research competitors on the web, especially if they are trying to decide what business they like best. They take the time to look you up, see what you are about, and compare you to other similar companies before deciding who gets their business. I highly recommend researching the multiple types of website design companies out there. If you have no idea how to create a website, then start small. WordPress, SquareSpace, Wix, Weebly, or Canva are great starting points. I use SquareSpace and it is pretty easy to update throughout the year with new photos or changes we have had in the business. They also make it easy to link your business email and workspace with the website. There are so many free tutorials on YouTube or on the website creation page. They also have templates already set up too. Use those. Heck, ask your friends and family if they can help you out. My 12 year old daughter could probably create a website. Kids these days I tell ya. But, if you do not feel comfortable doing this on your own, reach out to a marketing company who will charge by the hour to help you set up the website. This can get costly and there is not much in the $2000 budget for help, so if you can at least get started on your own and get a site up and running, you are halfway there.

You will also need to research domain sites. In order to create and keep your website name for example, www.acutedesigner.com, you have to register your website name and pay a monthly, or yearly fee to keep it. If you do not pay for it, your website will be shut down (no fun). There are several companies out there to use. Take your time to find the right fit. Squarespace offers domain registration so that might be a good fit to use their website as well. Network Solutions is another. The best thing to do is search all the ones out there and see what is the easiest to use or what feels right for you.

Contract Templates, Proposal Templates

Researching current contract templates and proposal templates are important to have in your back pocket in the beginning. These pieces are vital once you start getting clients. There are several free templates out there, just search. I also found quite a few templates that are available for purchase online through Etsy from $5-$15 each. They include the proposal template, contract, and a few other items. Personally, I wanted to save every penny and I created my own template based on the ones I found online. I used Google Docs/Sheets for both. If you have a better platform and want to get creative and keep things free, go for it!! But I will say it again, do not reinvent the wheel. In our day in age, we are blessed with the internet! See the breakdown of the two important docs you should have ready to go.

- **Proposals:** these are great because a lot of clients need an estimate with a breakdown of the costs before the project is started. This is also a way of starting the relationship with the client. It shows professionalism and gives them your word on pricing. ALWAYS under promise and over deliver!

- **Contracts:** this is a binding contract between you and client and outlines your expectations during the time your inventory is staged in a home. A contract also binds the client to agreeing what you are asking. On my contract, this is also where I ask for payment info. Very important so you can get paid for a job well done.

Local Real Estate Companies and Builders

Use your time now to research the local real estate companies in your area as well as the main builders in town. Make a list of the company, address, phone number. You will love yourself for doing this early so when you are ready to market the business and get your name out there, you already know who to target. For staging, we have narrowed down that our targeted clientele are realtors. Get to know them. Ask if you can host breakfast meetings, lunch meetings, etc. This is how you can get in front of more than one at a time. More on this in the marketing section.

Business Insurance Companies

Not all but most sellers or realtors will ask for a Certificate of Liability Coverage from your company before you get started on a project. This is normal, especially if you are new and the clients want peace of mind that things are covered in their homes if something were to be damaged by you, etc. It is important to research a few insurance companies around the area who cover businesses and understand business insurance. In the beginning, we paid minimal costs for insurance to keep within the budget. We made sure we had at least general liability and our inventory costs covered if there were ever damages. Glad we had this taken care of before our first job because the seller requested proof of insurance with our contract. Take the time to see what is offered and who will support you the best.

Marketing Companies

Now, you do not have to use a marketing company and pay someone to get you noticed. However, there are some great companies out there that are happy to help give advice on what you have created so far or provide fresh ideas on how to correctly use social media to your advantage. You do not have to use a local company. Most of the time, the marketing companies can find your social media, websites, etc online and help from afar so don't limit your search to just your city. If you want reassurance, research several companies and see if they are willing to charge an hourly rate to help. This will certainly keep costs down for you. The going rate is between $100-250 an hour. This is totally doable if you have done some leg work and come to the table with exact questions and help that you want to receive. Make your time with them worth it. BUT, do not feel like you need a marketing team at the very beginning business. It is important to look into companies and be prepared. Once you have several jobs under your belt and money in the bank, then see about spending on marketing help.

Accounting Firms/Accounting Software

Take some time here to check out the accountants in your area. These guys and gals are going to be your best help come tax time. As a business owner, you must file your 1099's by the end of January (if you employ contractors or extra help that get paid over $650 a year) and should have all tax docs in by February so there is ample time to get them filed in time for April. I am horrible at understanding taxes, even after 7 years of doing this I still heavily rely on my accountant to help me file. As an LLC, we pay between $750-$1000 for taxes in April when they are completed, but it is so worth it. So find and chat with several accountants to see if they understand small business taxes and can take on a new client. I interviewed three different companies face to face to get a sense of how they work and if they vibed with me. By doing this early on, you will feel confident when tax season arrives.

It is also imperative to research what software you want to use to keep your records, financials, invoices, payments, etc in order. There are several types out there. I started with Quickbooks because I was familiar with the software. They have a desktop version or an online version. If you have no clue what I am talking about, take time to research and understand the importance of documentation of your finances. Research: accounting software for small businesses. This will take you to multiple avenues for software. Some might be very simple to use and some might be difficult. But find one you feel works for you. I do know that online software starts around $10 a month and can go up from there. Just keep that in mind too. If you still are not sure what to do and you have already decided on an accountant, ask them what software they prefer to work with. That might help make your decision easier. Or if you picked a software already to use, ask the accountants if they are familiar with it and if not, then you know not to use them for your taxes.

Local Chamber of Commerce

Please take the time to look into your local Chamber of Commerce. I am so glad I was able to find out about them and their services. We have a great Chamber that offers multiple types of business classes, accounting classes, and networking groups to help support small business. While researching, I found out they had monthly breakfast meetings at different small business venues. This allows businesses that are members of the Chamber of Commerce to host the monthly breakfast and meet up at their space. What an awesome thing for the community to bring small business owners together. We went to several in the beginning of starting our business and met some amazing people. We gained several connections by going to these free breakfast meetups. Totally worth it.

I also found out that I could take an intro to business class through the Chamber for an 8 week session. A retired, successful business owner ran the class and I learned so much. This was super helpful since I was a newbie in business. So I highly recommend researching your local Chamber.

Chapter 2 Recap: Use this checklist to make sure you cover each section of research before moving on!

- Local Staging Companies
- Furniture/Accessories Costs
- Moving Companies/Storage Units
- Business Structures
- Secretary of State
- Business Plan/Mission Statement
- Websites/Domain
- Contracts/Proposals
- Local Real Estate Companies/Builders
- Business Insurance Companies
- Marketing Companies
- Accounting Firms/Accounting Software
- Local Chamber of Commerce

Chapter 3: First Things First.

Ready to get started building your business? This is the fun part. Now that you have done your research, let's jump in, create, and open up. This part at the beginning of building a business should feel exciting and get your creative juices flowing. If you start to feel overwhelmed or anxious, it is ok too, but push through those nervous thoughts. This is a new adventure and can feel daunting but I promise you, you are confident and have done all the necessary research to move forward. You got this!!

During this chapter, I will start calculating the startup costs when they are brought into the sections. I will add the cost at the bottom of the section. Then at the end of each chapter, I will total up the current costs just so you have a full understanding of where you stand. You will see these numbers in Chapter 3, 4, and 5 and with the grand total on startup costs at the bottom of Chapter 6. Please know that these prices are subject to change. Let's go!

Business Name

If you haven't been dreaming about what to call yourself yet, this is the time. Create your business name and have fun with it. When we got started, we created a list of about ten names that sounded fun and had purpose/significance to us. We looked into the meaning of the words that we wanted incorporated into the business name to see if they connected with who we were and wanted to express to the world. We also brainstormed logo designs at the same time too just to see if we could make a logo with that particular business name. Once we narrowed down the list to three, we went online to the Secretary of State website and checked to see if these names were already taken by other businesses in the state.

Be sure to have a few variations or options before deciding on the official name. How devastating to spend hours coming up with one name and then going to register the business and someone already has snagged that name up. Keep an open mind and give yourself a top three before finalizing. For example, we came up with "Acute Designs" and jumped on the web to register the name. Well, that name was taken by a marketing firm in the area. So we kept our minds open and easily changed "Designs" to "Designer". Easy. Plus I like Acute Designer better anyhow!

A few tips to think about when creating a business name. Try to think of the bigger picture. Think about the future of the business. Do you plan to stay in the same state the rest of the business' life or even expand out of the state or internationally? Then you might want to exclude the state you live in, in the name of your business. For example, if you live in Colorado, you might want to name the business Colorado Designs. What if you expand out of state? Then that name might not make sense if you expand into Florida. Or if you use your last name in the business name. What if you get married or get divorced? Always think bigger so you give your business room to grow!

**Total Cost: FREE

Business Logo

Get creative! Like I mentioned previously, when we started exploring business names, we also played around with the logo designs to make sure we could coordinate the two. There are a lot of ways you can create your logo. You could either draw out your own logo or use computer software, or free online software to make it happen. We ended up using www.canva.com to create our logo. Canva is a wonderful tool that you can either use for free with limited services or pay a monthly fee for unlimited services. When we first started, we of course sought out the free version and created a simple yet effective logo.

If you draw out your logo, be sure to take a clear picture of it with your camera so you can download it to your computer to upload to social media sites, website, marketing, etc. You could also scan it on a printer to upload to the computer as well. The biggest thing is to make your logo digital and easily accessible for online use since we live in a digital world!

You could also use a basic software program already installed on your computer like Microsoft Word or Publisher or Apple Pages or Graphic. Don't feel like you have to get fancy. A simple logo can be a classic design that stays with you for the life of the business.

When creating a logo, be sure to design something that can be replicated in a cost effective way. For example, don't use too many details and colors. Come time to buy business cards, or marketing materials, too many details and colors can be expensive and sometimes too hard to add to a pen or notepad for marketing items and swag.

Total Cost: FREE

Business Address

You will need to decide on a physical mailing address. The state and federal government need to know how to find you. To save money in the beginning, we did not rent out a warehouse or commercial building. We started out of our homes. Because of this, I did not want to use my personal home address and have random potential clients showing up at my own home. My business partner was also onboard to find another solution. So we did a quick search for a PO BOX set up. Did you know UPS stores have mailboxes that you can rent each month and not have a PO Box address?? We were able to gain a mailing address with a "Suite" rather than a "Box". This makes it sounds more professional and allows us to get mail in a central location. Yes, we do have those potential clients who find us online and want to physically meet us at our "office". I know this could be a negative for some, however, I have found out a lot of these potential clients end up being people who want to sell us things rather than need our services. If they really need us, they will call or email. I have let this "loss" go over the years and realize I can focus more on my regular clients instead. To have our PO Box/Suite address, we do pay around $25 a month. Totally worth it. **Side note: Be sure to keep record of this payment, especially if you haven't set up your business checking account yet. Always keep documents of money spent so you can deduct expenses at the end of the year.

However, if you want to at least start out with a personal address to get the business up and running, feel free to do so. Just know that you will probably have to pay a fee to update a change of address with the state. Each state is different. For example, when I need to make a change, I pay $10 each time to file an address change to the Secretary of State website for the state of Colorado.

***Total Cost: FREE to $25 a month**

Register with the State

Now that you have your list of business names, it is time to get registered with the state so you can lock in your business name before anyone can take it! It is also important to do this before you create an email address, website, etc. You don't want to take the time to get everything else done and then have to start over because the business name you picked is already in use.

- **How to Register with the State:**

    It's a good thing you already did the research on where to go to set up your business with the state, right?! But just in case you need a refresher, follow along.

    To register, go to the Secretary of State website and in the search tab (usually located on the top of the main page) type in "business search" or "business database". You are essentially trying to find out if the business name you want is in use or open for you to use. Each state is different but this type of search should get you what you are looking for. If you search the state website and your ideal business name is not in use, then get registered!

Be sure you are registering under the correct type of business. If you want to be an LLC, then find the form to register an LLC. I did the research only on LLC formation so if you need info on how to register as another type of business then give your state secretary a call. They should be able to help you! Back to LLC. Depending on where you are, the costs of registering an LLC differ between states. See below costs for a few different states that I researched. On average, the fee ranged between $100-300. Sorry Massachusetts, you came out the most expensive with a whopping $500 fee. Don't hold that against me!! Either way, you can always find the exact cost of your state on your Secretary of State website. Please remember these prices are subject to change.

- **Origination Fee to Form an LLC:**
    - Colorado $50
    - New York $200
    - Texas $300
    - Florida $125
    - California $70
    - Massachusetts $500

FYI, there will always be an annual or biennial Periodic Report you must file (typically due on the date you formed the business with the state) to keep your business in good standing with the state. On average for the states listed above, the report cost is between $10-$800 each report. California was the highest cost that I found and done biennially at $800. Here in Colorado, we pay $10 every year for our periodic report. If you haven't already researched your state, be sure to do so when registering your business so you know when to pay that cost and for how much! **Side note: I do not have the Periodic Report cost included in the startup costs below but be sure to budget those costs because it will come up at certain times of the year based on your state.

- **Operating Agreement/Partnership Agreement**

    If you are registering as an LLC whether it is a Single-Member LLC, Partnership, or forming an LLC with more than two members, I highly recommend that you create your operating agreement during this time in order to file with the state or with a bank to open up a checking account. If you did not research these earlier, take a look online or on www.sba.gov website for examples and templates.

- **Articles of Organization**

    This is a great time to also create your Articles of Organization as well in order to file with the state and have it ready for your bank when opening your accounts. Again, this is a simple document that shows your intent to create an LLC with your state.

***Total Cost: $50-$500 for startup registration fee*

Register with the Federal Government

Now that you have registered your business with the state, the next step is to register with the IRS so you can retrieve a tax id number or EIN. This will be important to obtain in order to file for taxes at the end of the year, open a business account with a bank, register for insurance for the business, and register for a business license or permit if need be. To register, go to www.irs.gov. On their homepage, click the link "Apply for an Employer ID Number EIN".

This will take you step by step to file with the IRS. Be sure to keep this number in a safe place as well as the document. You will need this document when opening up a bank account and applying for insurance and everything else!

***Total Cost: FREE*

Open Up a Checking Account

Now that you are registered with the state and federal government, time to get your checking account open so you can get the business up and running. There are several important things on the list to open up and get for the business so you can look and act professional and start collecting income!! If you have a trusted bank already in the area, use them to set up the business account. If not, see what banks are in the area that you can access easily and gain online access through. It makes all the difference in the world if the bank you chose is easy to work with both in person and online. **Side note: Make sure to open this account before you purchase anything for your business. This makes it so simple to keep all expenses under the same account. It will also make your accounting much easier to document everything spent and when tax season arrives, all your expenses are in one place and one account. The only things you should purchase without this account is your registration cost to open up the business with the secretary of state and a possible "business" address. Just be sure to provide the documentation of these expenses to your accountant at tax time.

What you need to open an account:

- Business EIN number
- Proof that you are registered with the state. Use the document showing paid and registered with the secretary of state
- 2 other forms of identification like driver's license or passport
- Business Address
- Operating Agreement
- Articles of Organization
- $2500 minus the registration fee and address fee (if applicable) you spent from your personal account

You might want to purchase checks at first but it is not necessary. We used the checks to pay ourselves for the paper trail but again it is up to you how you want to pay yourself and pay for expenses. A book of checks can range from $25-50. You could also request a few checks to start with so you are not spending extra on a book of checks. Most banks will give you several for free. Also in the beginning, you could get charged a monthly fee if you do not have a certain amount of money kept in the checking account. This monthly fee is typically $15 a month but check with your bank and see what they offer or if they would be willing to give you a few months with a waiver charge or exemption to get on your feet. With our bank, if we can maintain $2500 in our checking account at all times, we do not pay a monthly fee. Or, if we use our credit card that we opened up with the checking account for expenses, then we were able to waive the monthly fee. **Side note: If you do get a credit card with your checking account, ALWAYS pay off your card every month. If not, this can take you down a debt rabbit hole you DO NOT want to go down. Anyhow, check with your bank on options so you have the best set up for your accounts. This is also the time to deposit your remainder of cash up to $2500. Whatever you have left from the $2500, deposit with your bank so you can start paying for your expenses on the business account.

***Total Cost: FREE to $50 to start/ Up to $15 a month if requirements are not met*

Get Business Insurance

Once you have your bank account ready to go, the next step is to add insurance for your business. To start, you can either set up an appointment to meet in person with an insurance agent who understands business insurance or set it up over the phone. You will need documentation to give to the insurance agent so be prepared either way. Typically, the easiest way to start out with the business is to have a General Liability of Insurance to cover you in someone else's home as well as cover your things if something happens while the items are in your client's home. Ask your insurance agent what would be the best way to cover you in the most basic type of insurance. Also ask them if they are able to provide the Proof of Insurance quickly if any of your clients request it. It is also important that the agent understands how you use your business and what it entails so again you are covered fully. To prepare, have a statement ready to explain how your services are used. Below are some other things that you will need to help set up the insurance for your business.

What you need to provide to your agent:

- Proof that you are registered with the state.
- Business EIN Number
- Business Address
- 2 Forms of Identification
- A Description of the Business and services

***Total Cost: $50-$85 a month for basic insurance costs*

Business Plan/Mission Statement

Let's be honest, writing a business plan seems overwhelming and not part of the fun of starting a business. I do not expect you to create the entire business plan at the very beginning, or heck even start one, however, it is essential to decide on your values and where you see the future of the business before you take off. The most important part of creating a business is to look at the heart and soul of how you want to be of service to your community and how you can help add growth to your area and yourself over the years.

Make it easy on yourself and start with a mission statement and then if you want to create a simple business plan, then create the Lean Startup Plan so you have the key elements of the business in writing. By doing these steps, you will have a written down plan of: your values, what services your company will be providing, how you want to present yourself to the community, how you add value to the community, how you project your growth, and how you see the future of the business. The beauty of all this, if you start to feel lost during the process or having a hard month, go back to your plan/statement. Go back to where it started and reflect on how excited you were to begin this venture. Go back to how you originally wanted to serve the community. This will rejuvenate your energy and push you to make it through the tough times. Owning a business isn't easy. I have had those days and weeks where I just feel burnt out and lost. But, by taking the time to stop and reevaluate my business plan/statement and think of all my wins (big and small) made all the difference and brought me back to life. It reminded me of the girl boss that I am and that I am here to serve. So just do it. Get the business plan or mission statement going so you have a place to start, a place to grow, a place to reflect.

Total Cost: FREE

Staging Proposal/Contract

It is important to create templates for your proposals and contracts in advance before you get your first job so you are ready and prepared and do not have to create something last minute. Again, there are lots of free templates out there on the internet that you can replicate on Google Docs, or Microsoft Word, or Pages. If you do not want to replicate these, then you can find preset templates on Etsy where you literally just type in your business name info and logo. These typically run from $5-20 dollars depending on the amount you want to purchase. I kept our costs at zero by researching the templates I want and taking a few hours to replicate them on Google Docs and Google Sheets to make them our own.

When it comes to the contract, make sure your wording is to your liking and that you explain in detail your expectations. Contracts are the binding agreement between you and your client. Make sure your clients know and understand what to expect when you show up in the home and what will happen if there is damage on your part or their part. Be specific so there are no assumptions. Make sure you have on the contract the cost and for how long that cost is good for. Be sure your business is covered and you look out for yourself while also being respectful to the property and your clients. I also recommend having a lawyer or paralegal overlook your contract to make sure it is in good standing and you have your i's dotted and t's crossed. If you can, ask a family member or friend who understands legal documents to look over it. This kept our initial costs free but it is super important to have some professional read through it so you are covered later down the road. If you don't know anyone, ask an attorney if they would charge an hourly fee to look it over. This could cost around $250-$350 but could be highly valuable so you don't lose money in the long run.

***Total Cost: FREE for initial setup*

Meet with a CPA

Now that you have your ducks in a row and have the most crucial parts of the business set and ready, this could be a good time for you to start meeting with a CPA to establish your relationship and confirm they are able to take you on as a new client.

Hopefully you had the time early on to do the research on the accountants in the area and found one or two you want to interview if you haven't already. Be sure to take this step early on so you are not struggling at the beginning of tax season trying to find someone willing to take on a business account at the last minute. Most accounting firms are too busy to accept new business clients right before tax season starts. Be sure to meet with them in the summer, fall, or winter to set up your info. This is also a good time to confirm what type of accounting software they prefer to use or can easily access to help with taxes.

Usually the first visit with the CPA is free to meet and establish the relationship. Next steps typically include the accounting firm emailing over a portal invite so you know where to upload tax documents.

If you want an accountant to help you set up your accounting software, they will charge an hourly fee to do so, usually between $250-350 an hour. If you can, avoid this cost and watch youtube videos on how to set everything up or most of the time, the software company will have free help with set up. Use these tools to your advantage. It will save time and money and remember we want to keep our costs low in the beginning!!

***Total Cost: FREE for initial set-up*

Select an Accounting Software Program

Now you are ready to set up your software for accounting. It is important to do this early on so you can start including expenses and income in an easy way. You should have researched which software you would prefer to use and which ones your accountant is familiar with. If not, look now. We use Quickbooks Online and are very happy with the program. There are many other programs: Zoho Books, Sage, FreshBooks, Zero, Quicken and many more. They have a starting price around $15 a month to use. They are all pretty straightforward to use, Quickbooks Online being the most comprehensive as an online program. Use what is best for your business but keep it simple so it is easy for you to update every week. Once you pick the software, they all have videos or guides to help you get everything set up.

How many times to update throughout the month? You make that call. In the beginning, your expenses and income might be slow and it's ok if you update or track your spending once a month but just be sure to keep up with your tracking. Once things pick up, it can be easy to forget to add in items and track consistently so be sure to pick a day or days through the month to stay on top of the accounting. You will also want to reconcile your accounts each month to "settle" the expenses and income. Stay on top of this so your books are clean for tax season. Again tons of videos and help with each software program!

You might not want to set up the software but it is so important to have it ready to go. The more you are ready and set in the beginning, the easier it will be to follow through and be prepared for taxes at the end of the year.

***Total Cost: $15 to $30 a month*

***GRAND TOTAL FOR ALL ITEMS: Up to $690 depending on your state*

Starting Investment: $2,500

                                                   -$ 690 Startup Costs

                                                   $1,810 Remaining

***These prices are subject to change.*

Chapter 3 Recap: Use this checklist to make sure you cover each section before moving on!

- Create Business Name
- Create Business Logo
- Decide on Business Address
- Register Business with the State
- Register Business with the Federal Government
- Open Checking Account
- Get Business Insurance
- Write Business Plan/Mission Statement
- Create Business Contract/Proposal Template
- Meet with CPA
- Get Accounting Software

Chapter 4: Make An Appearance Online.

It is now time to make your business known! Any successful business these days has easy access online to its clients whether that is via a website or social media. It is so important to have both for any new business taking off. Everyone starts with their phones or tablets to find resources these days so get out there for them to find you!

Business Website/Domain Name/Email Address

THIS IS CRUCIAL!!!! No questions asked, you have to have a presence online if you want to own a successful business. That means a website. You have done the research on which creator you want to use and what domain company, so now create.

Domain Name

Getting a domain name/website name goes hand in hand with a website. You have to have a domain name before you start your site. This again is your website name, like www.acutedesigner.com. Once you pick out the domain provider you would like to use for your website and your actual domain name, get registered. The average cost for keeping your domain name is about $10-20 a year. This cost will keep your domain name locked and not allow others to steal your website name. DO NOT let this go by the wayside. If you forget to pay for this, you could potentially lose your website name and your website. Automate the payment or write down all the info and keep it somewhere special so you do not forget!!

**Total Cost: $10-20 a year*

Business Email

It is so important to have a business email to send out marketing info and receive emails in a professional manner. We went with Square Space for our website and they offer Google/Gmail for our email. I like Gmail because we also use the Google Suite and write our consultation reports with Google Sheets and use Google Docs for contracts. We end up paying for our emails through our website since SquareSpace teamed up with Google Suite. It is not necessary to pay for an email address but it is a small cost included in the monthly website managing fee more times out of ten. It also allowed us to use our business name in the email rather than have a basic @gmail.com or @aol.com, etc. ending. Choose what works best for you. We also created an email that was easy to remember and to tell our clients! For example, amy@acutedesigner.com. Simple, sweet, and quick to give out. I am also glad I went this route for my email address and only used my first name because I got married at the start of the business. This is another place to think about the bigger picture and keep things basic and simple.

**Total Cost: Included in Website Fee or FREE*

Website

Now that your domain name is set, get going on your site! This should be a fun and exciting time to use your creative juices. Find an easy layout to start with and stick to the basics in the beginning. **Side note: I am a perfectionist and started getting razor focused on the details of the beginnings of our website. BAD IDEA!! That can take you down a long rabbit hole of wasted time. You just need to get the website in motion so potential clients can find you! Over the years, I have learned to set aside time each quarter to reanalyze the site and adjust what needs to be adjusted. For example, I add new pictures to the portfolio or make each page more streamline and not over complicated. The beauty of technology is that you can always change what you don't like on your website.

What to include on the website

- **Home Page:** this gives a general statement about who you are and what you offer

- **About Us/Me:** this gives a background of your experience and a simple statement of why you do what you do

- **Services Page:** this breaks down your services in detail (some will include starting out pricing here or others will create a tab to email for pricing)

- **Portfolio:** to get the attention of any potential client, you must show them your work and this is a huge marketing tool on your website

- **Contact Us/Me:** this page usually is simple and straight to the point but shows clients your contact info and other pages might have links to this page so the clients will be directed to submit contact into in the same spot on your website

- **Social Media:** this page will link your social media account and if clients click here, it takes them directly to your social media. (not everyone does this but it does allow clients to see your day to day work so you do not have to update your website every week with new photos)

- **Blog:** this page is important to include and add to regularly. Potential clients want to read articles about great expert advice on home staging, decorating, adding value to real estate, etc. Having a blog creates a fun and exciting way to market who you are and can allow you to increase traffic flow to your website through search engines. Blogs also help build trust with your clients with your posts and add insightful info.

Tips for your website

- Include tabs to other pages on your homepage to make it easier for clients to access your info in a quick and simple manner. For example, under a simple explanation or photo of what services you have, you could add a link for clients to click and it would take them directly to the services page for more detail.

- Be sure to have your phone number and email address on every page to make it easy for clients to reach you. Always give clients an opportunity to reach you on every page. When the website is simple and easy to use, the clients will keep using it and stay on it longer!

- Keep the backdrop and font simple. Make the website easy to read and easy to follow or potential clients will move on to another company's website.

- Make the website easy for YOU to adjust and change throughout the course of the business. If you make it too difficult, you will never want to take the time to update it and make it better.

- Once you have the website almost where you want it, try opening the website on a computer, a phone, or a tablet. Every device opens your website differently. It could look amazing on a computer and then when you open it up on a phone, it could look like pure dog poop. Yes, I found that one out personally and too late. I spent so much time testing it out on the computer, that I forgot the most important thing, the phone. I ended up spending many more hours adjusting the site and layout of pictures and wording. Remember, almost everyone has a smart phone these days and usually starts their searches for companies/business, on those devices. If you don't have an easy to use website, they are on to the next business within 30 seconds.

- Portfolio pics-how do you make this page look great before you even get your first job? Use your friends and family!! We were so fortunate to use my brother's house to stage and accessorize his place. We used his furniture and rugs and art but rearranged everything and added our touches to the rooms. We took pictures (ALOT) and enhanced the photos to look their best for the website. Ask your friends, family, neighbors, therapists, trainers, whoever you have in your life to help you get started. 9 times out of 10, people will help out and enjoy a restyle to their home!

Cost of a Website:

Since you did your previous research, you should already have an idea of what it will cost per month to run the website. BUT, if you got a little eager and just went for it, now it's time to check out the cost. Most websites will charge a monthly fee to run the site online. This is a basic charge and totally worth it so you can always be online. Monthly costs usually run from $30-50 a month. That is just to keep the website online. Most websites will also include your email address access in the monthly charge too. Just a little tip, have it automatically withdrawn so you never have a hold on your site. Makes life simple and when you start getting busy, you don't have to worry if that bill is paid or not.

**Total Cost: $30-50 a month

Business Social Media Accounts

Along with keeping up to date on a website, you must also have a presence on social media platforms too. I have had quite a few realtors find me on Instagram and we now have a great, working relationship. It does take some time to manage the social media pages but it's totally worth it in today's modern society.

To start, create a Facebook page and Instagram page. These are your basics and it's important to have both. On the bright side, Meta(who owns both platforms) has a business app where you can manage both accounts at the same time and schedule posts just once to hit both sites at the same time.

This has saved me hours over the years because I can batch content and just let it roll.

You can also have a twitter account and whatever else is out there but keep it simple. Running a business is hard enough. Don't add too much stress to your life if your day ends up filled with hours of social media posting and not focusing on the business itself. NOT WORTH IT. You want to be out staging and decorating and loving the life of a home stager!

Tips for Successful Social Media:

- Make sure your website, email, and phone number are easily accessible on all platforms. It is so important for your potential clients to have easy access to connect with you or what's the point of having a social media account.

- Link your personal accounts with the business accounts so more and more friends, family, and potential clients can find you. Friendly reminder: Be sure to clean up your personal accounts and not have old fraternity pictures posted from the time you did a keg stand. I mean I guess you could leave it up there for giggles but potential clients might be a little hesitant about trying out your business.

- Follow as many realtors, flippers, builders, even interior designers, and of course home stagers. I follow quite a few stagers and they follow back. It's great because we all constantly compliment each other. The more you follow, the more your name gets out and realtors (your main client) can see you are around and what you do.

- Post various types of items. Post pictures or videos or stories. The more things are varied, the better. You also want to try different perspectives of posts. Close ups are fun, multiple rooms, one room focus, and before and afters are amazing. Get silly with the posts too. We have done a few while drinking champagne on a back deck with our exterior furniture in the shot. The more interesting, the better. You will keep a captive audience. **Side note: ChatGPT can help with content. This is a great way to use technology to your advantage. ChatGPT can be very useful when creating content and can make your life easier as well as allow you to spend less time figuring out what to post online. I could write an entire book on how to use ChatGPT so I suggest looking into it and see how it can benefit your business!

- Batch content. This means after collecting multiple pictures and videos of current jobs and projects, schedule multiple posts to get you through the week or a few weeks at a time. I learned the hard way and posted the morning I wanted the post to show online and would always end up posting too late in the day and not getting enough views. There are logarithms based on where you live and what times of days people like to view social media. Research your area to see when the most active time frame people are on social media. That's when you want to schedule your posts. For example, I schedule my posts for 10 am on Tuesdays and Thursdays every week and I do at least four posts batched at a time so I am not always trying to post things at the last minute. It definitely helps.

- Post at least twice a week. The more you post, the better. It is important to stay active on your social media so more and more can follow you and see your content. It would be great if you could post everyday and maybe you could start that way but I find it easier and more attainable to keep to 2 days a week. Again, don't reinvent the wheel and use the scheduling part of the app so you can focus more on growing the business in other ways.

- Use hashtags. When I post, I always include several popular hashtags. What are hashtags you ask? Hashtags increase brand awareness, expands your audience, increases engagement, boosts discovery, and follows trends. These are all important when building your business. In social media platforms, users can actually use the key words in hashtags to search specific words used in that hashtag. For example, #interior design will take the user to all posts including that tagline/hashtag. So if you add that hashtag on your post, more users can find you that way. In the Meta App, there's a way to input the hashtags you want and save them so they are always there. Research trending hashtags in your local area so you can include these on your posts and widen your audience. #awesome #girlboss #you get the picture

****Total Cost: FREE*

GRAND TOTAL FOR ALL ITEMS: Up to $70

Starting Investment:

$2,500

-$ 690 Startup Costs

$1,810 Remaining

$ 70 Website/Domain Costs

$1,740 Remaining

**These prices are subject to change.

Chapter 4 Recap: Use this checklist to make sure you cover each section before moving on!

- Get Domain Name
- Get Website
- Setup Email Address
- Set up Website
- Set up Social Media Accounts

Chapter 5: Market the Hell Out of Yourself.

I think this is one of the hardest parts of starting out a business but one of the most important in order to create and establish clientele. If no one knows who you are, you must put yourself out there in the community and get noticed. This can be daunting and scary but you have to put your big girl panties on and push yourself out of your comfort zone. Now is the time to market to realtors, builders, and flippers. You have done the research on who is out there, so now it's time to make contact and show them who you are and how you can help them grow their business too with a great partnership!

Marketing Materials

There are a few marketing materials that are essential to having in the beginning so you can leave an impression on your potential clients. Business cards are vital as well as brochures that can help paint a picture about who you are and what services you can provide to your potential clients. There are several ways you can create both business cards and brochures and keep costs down to a minimum.

Business cards
- **What essentials to add on a business card:** business name, your name, business address, email, website, phone number, business logo, and social media accounts

- Create the business cards on your computer using templates found on either Microsoft or Pages. Google Docs has templates too. You could also use free software like Canva or Adobe and create a business card from their many free templates. If you already have a great working printer with ink, just purchase card stock which is around $5-7 and print the business cards from home. This will be a huge savings. Yes, the cards won't be of professional quality, but they will get your name out there to start.

- If you need to purchase ink to print off the cards, then it might be more cost effective to have a printing store print them out for you for a much lower rate since ink for printers can be more expensive than the printer itself! If you would rather go straight to a company that prints the business cards on professional grade cards, there are several companies out there. Vistaprint, Zazzle, Office Depot, and even Canva will print out cards for you and ship to your home. You can use their many styles of templates and get a pack of 50-100 cards. Just doing a quick search, Office Depot offers 50 business cards starting at $11.99! But most of these companies will charge around $15-$30.

***Total Cost: $12-$30 for 50-100 cards*

Brochures

- **What essentials to add on a brochure:** business name, your name, business address, email, website, phone number, business logo, social media accounts, about you section, about your services section, before and after photos, photos of best work so far

(remember these photos can be from friends and families homes)

- When creating the content for the brochure, be sure to think how your services will benefit your future clients. This is a quick way to market directly to your clients. They need to see a reason to use your services in the first place and try you out. Use short and sweet phrases and data to showcase the importance of staging a home.

- Just like business cards, you can create brochures on your computer using existing templates. Canva and Adobe also have great templates. We personally used a free template off Canva to create our brochure and then took the saved document and printed it with Vistaprint. You could also take the saved document from Canva and print it at home. Office Depot or Staples can even print them on professional paper too. Brochures are a little more expensive because you want to capture the beauty of the photos included on the brochure. For a box of 25, they can range around $30 and up to $75 for a box of 50.

**Total Cost: $30 for 25/ $75 for 50*

Free Food Talks

You now have your marketing materials and are ready to get out there in the world. One easy way to get in front of a lot of real estate agents all at the same time, is to host a breakfast or lunch at one of their weekly or monthly morning meetings at their main office. This can be beneficial for your business. Call around to the real estate companies and see if they would be willing to let you host one of their meetings. This means that you would bring in food and drinks for the realtors to enjoy while participating in their meeting.

Typically the firm will give you about 5 to 10 minutes to speak to all of the realtors about who you are and what you offer. Be sure to leave a few minutes for questions and feedback. The firm might even allow you to leave your business cards and brochures in their office for the realtors who did not make it to the meeting. Now, you might not get a ton of new contacts at once, however, look at this type of marketing a success if you can get one realtor on board. You work with that realtor once and do a great job, guarantee, they talk about you to their colleagues. This will eventually create a domino effect. Word of mouth is powerful so finding just one realtor to please will grow tenfold over the years and make all this effort worthwhile.

Tips for a Successful Meeting

- **Have enough food:** Realtors are always on the go so when they get a chance to sit down and have a snack, they will take it! Make sure you ask the person in charge of the meetings about the average attendance to the meetings. Take that number and multiply by 20%. You never want to run out of food! Ask the company if they provide the coffee or drinks or anything else for their meetings. Do not assume anything. You want to make sure you have something to wash down your yummy delights so always ask and prepare. Don't forget the utensils, plates, and napkins if the real estate company does not provide any extras. Also make sure to have gluten free options and a variety of food for all to enjoy.

- **Have enough materials:** It is important to have enough marketing material to leave for all the realtors. Use the 20% rule here as well. Any leftover materials could be left at the company by request for other realtors who did not make it to the meeting or even newcomers too.

- **Be prepared:** Sometimes at these meetings, there is a projector set up and could potentially be used by you to showcase your website or before and after photos. HOWEVER, technology does not always work when you want it, so be prepared to just speak to the group and let the brochures give a pretty picture of who you are. We learned this the hard way and technology failed us, so we went on a whim and just spoke about the biz as best as possible. Luckily we had our marketing materials in front of the realtors.

- **What to say:** It can be nerve-wracking speaking in front of people you do not know so have a guideline prepped for what you want to cover. Start with who you are and your background. Explain your services and what you can offer them. Give them quick points about how your services can benefit them and how staging can add value to their listings. Give a general cost of your services. Provide your service area as well because realtors work all over the place! Remind them about the brochure in front of them and where they can find you (website, social, etc.). Always end with a chance for them to ask you questions.

- **Have a calendar ready:** You might even get a "bite" at that very meeting and a realtor could use your services right away. Again be prepared and have your calendar and schedule ready to go so you can be sure to get started.

**Total Cost: $100-150 for food and paper products

Free Online Business Directories

Online business directories are another great way to attract and market to new clients. They catch the attention of those searching directly for your type of services. The best part about this, is that they are free to set up! There are several websites where you can market your business online for free and I highly suggest adding your business to all of them in order to increase your visibility online. With most of these directories, you are able to add photos, link your website and social media platforms, and get reviews. The most impactful directories are below:

- Google My Business
- Yelp
- Big Places for Businesses
- Local.com
- BBB or Better Business Bureau
- YP or Yellow Pages
- Nextdoor
- Facebook Business Pages
- Linkedin Business Pages
- Foursquare

***Total Cost: FREE*

Blogging with Social Media Accounts

Blogging or Vlogging are fabulous marketing tools that can enhance your visibility online and create trust with potential clients. Blogging can be very important to businesses because it helps provide fresh content on a website and can increase more traffic to a website. According to HubSpot Marketing, businesses with blogs get 55% more website visitors than those without blogs. Regular blogging can also help with SEO rankings as well as increase brand awareness and even generate leads. Potential clients might see one of your articles and want to know more about the business. Adding this type of content to your website also can showcase your expertise in an area and attract more leads. It is another way to also add content to your social media accounts.

In the beginning, we started blogging regularly on our website and included fun tips about design and staging to increase interest in our business. We kept most of the articles simple and an easy, quick read. We incorporated wording in the article to include our location and important key features to associate us with design and staging. Most importantly, we had fun writing the articles and sharing our wisdom with our community. Once the articles were finished, we would then be sure to add to our social media accounts when a new blog dropped. This is important because it not only ties your website and socials together but brings more visibility to both types of accounts. An easy and free way to market to your potential clients.

As mentioned before in the previous chapter, social media accounts are a great way to market your business and for free! Continue to post at least 2 times a week. Include your location and hashtags. Change up the content if you are able and have fun with what you post. You would be surprised at how many people can see your posts and how much you can drive more traffic to your website and business.

****Total Cost: FREE*

Email Marketing

Email marketing is another great tool for free advertising for your business. It is a way to retain loyal clients, keep them informed, and even conduct surveys. You are able to tailor your content to your clients and improve your brand recognition. Believe it or not, this could help increase sales and even drive more traffic to your website.

The most important thing is to make sure the emails actually benefit your clients and give them solid information so they want to take the time to read them. Emails could be sent monthly or quarterly. They could include seasonal tips on what to do in your home or how to stage a certain area in the home. They could include the latest design trend or paint color of the year. They could include promotions or coupons. The emails could be a survey of what your readers want to see. It is all about keeping them engaged and wanting more from the "staging expert". **Side note: Just be careful not to use this tactic as a way to ask for sales. That could be a turnoff to your clients.

****Total Cost: FREE*

Buddy up with your Local Chamber of Commerce

When starting out a new business with little to no clientele, find time to get to know your local Chamber of Commerce. They can be a huge asset when marketing your business. You do not have to join the commerce at first but find out what they are about and how they can help the small businesses in their town/city. Most chambers will gladly invite you to one of their monthly meetings so you have the ability to see what they do and help guide you on how they could be a benefit to your business. As I mentioned in the research section, someone from the chamber could also offer you an invite to one of their monthly breakfast meetings that are typically hosted at an active chamber of commerce member's place of business. The breakfast meetings are great. This is an easy and free way to market yourself to the locals. These meetings really allow you to mingle and make connections with the local businesses in the area. We met so many amazing people and found a few potential businesses to partner up with for our business needs. We went to several after being offered an invite to go. We did not want to take advantage of the chamber of commerce so we only went to the meetings when we were asked by local chamber partners. If you start showing up to every event and meeting, then you will definitely have to join! **Side note: Always have business cards and brochures on hand at these meetings. We gave out a dozen business cards in one meeting and a few brochures. Glad we had them on hand!

***Total Cost: FREE*

Check out your Local Real Estate Staging Associations or Realtor Associations

I wish I would have known about RESA when I first started the business! RESA is the Real Estate Staging Association and is nationwide. They are a group that links professional stagers across the US as well as provides education and business tools to active members. If new realtors or sellers are looking for stagers and not sure where to go, they can find local stagers in the area on RESA's website. I highly recommend looking into them. It will be another avenue for marketing yourself in your area but also finding a local community of stagers to lean on when you need advice. You will want to join the national chapter as well as the local chapter. Dues are annual and run $190 for the national chapter and around $50 for the local chapter. Now, we are trying to start this business for $2500 and thrive so I suggest looking into the association so you have an idea of how they can help. However, hold off on paying the dues until you know you have the funds. Get the important things taken care of first!

Another agency to look into is the Realtor Association. In Denver, there are two branches because the city is so large. This is an association of realtors but they also look for local companies who could be a big asset to support the realtors throughout the city. Stagers are a big resource for realtors so look into being a sponsored company. This does include an annual fee but puts your name out to your potential clients. We did not join until a few years after starting so we could make sure costs were low in the beginning. Annual dues can be estimated around $1500-2000. These dues are quite expensive but could make a big difference for your growth. I do recommend trying it out if you have the funds but if you are not gaining potential clients through this resource then be sure to opt out the following year to save money.

***Total Cost: FREE to look into it*

Branch Out to Family and Friends Around Town

When starting out a new business, the biggest supporters are your family and friends. Reach out to them to help share the word you are in town and ready to serve. This is the easiest and cheapest way to market yourself. Have family and friends share your posts on social media. If you are able to use their homes to stage a room or rooms for both marketing photos and experience, have them leave reviews online about how you did to help build your exposure and online presence. If they have a local business and have space in their building/office, give them your merch/marketing items and leave business cards or brochures in lunch rooms, or the reception desk. This type of marketing is the best because it is word of mouth and 9 times out of 10, it's all positive.

The most important thing when working with your family and friends is to prepare them with the right wording and phrases to spread correct and helpful information about your business. See below on some easy tips.

Tips for Successful Marketing with Family and Friends:

- **Practice before you tell the world:** I know this sounds crazy but prepare a checklist of items you want to express about your new business. Who you are, how you can serve and benefit the community, when you are open for business, etc. I know these are your family and friends you are going to be chatting with, but if you can come off professional and prepped, they will be impressed and confident that you won't let down their friends and colleagues they are spreading the word to.

- **Keep it simple:** When explaining your business to family and friends, keep the lingo and info simple. I find it overwhelming when I am thrown a lot of information about something new so use your checklist to go over key points about the business. This will allow family and friends to remember how to market you in the best light.

- **Give them three:** Along with keeping it simple, only give a few main points to your peeps so they can relay the info back correctly and eagerly.

- **Be enthusiastic:** Be excited about the new venture! When you are confident and eager to start helping the community, others see it and feel it. This will put pep in their step to happily shout your name from the rooftops.

- **Ask for feedback:** Once your family and friends have had some time to start sharing the word, ask them how it is going. Ask them if anyone has seemed interested or asked about more on who you are. This is a good sign that they could possibly need your services. If you feel comfortable, ask for contact info from the potential client to start a working relationship.

- **Give incentives**: Sometimes family and friends are not always as excited to share the news to fellow friends and colleagues. It's ok, entice them. Barter their time with helping in their home, redecorate a space or give them design time and advice. You could also give them an incentive for like $50 if you can gain a client and stage job from their marketing help. Or shoot, a case of beer could be enticing enough (I know my husband will do anything for beer!)

**Total Cost: FREE

SEO-To use or not to use

Another way of increasing your exposure and online presence, is to pay for a company to enhance the SEO on your website and social media. SEO quite simply is Search Engine Optimization. Now, I know this can really help get your ratings up and push you to the top of the Google searches, BUT it is not cheap. To start the business and maximize your spending and profit, wait on this service. I think you can definitely look into SEO companies and see how they could boost your business but wait until you can afford this and are making a profit. We are almost to our 8 year mark in the business and I have yet to use their services. We decided as a business to grow organically and not overwhelm ourselves with higher demand. This has worked for us. I did however, reach out to a marketing firm recently, and paid an hourly fee of $100 to help get advice on SEO. This allowed me to learn how to change wording and other items on our website and social media platforms without using a third party company. Now I adjust those things on my own when needed. Worth the money to pay for an hour of an expert's time! BUT…in the beginning, keep this cost at $0! Youtube, Google, ChatGPT are amazing resources to help you understand what you can do right now without additional costs.

Total Cost: FREE for the initial set-up

***GRAND TOTAL FOR ALL ITEMS: $255**

Starting Investment:

$2,500

-$ 690 **Startup Costs**

$1,810 Remaining

$ 70 **Website/Domain Costs**

$1,740 Remaining

$ 255 **Marketing Material Costs**

$1,485 Remaining

**These prices are subject to change.*

Chapter 5 Recap: Use this checklist to make sure you cover each section before moving on!

- Create Market Materials
- Host Breakfast or Lunch at Realtor Firm
- Check out Local Chamber of Commerce
- Setup Business on Online Websites like Google or Linked In
- Check into Realtor Associations or Staging Associations
- Branch out to Family and Friends Around Town
- Create Email Marketing Tools
- Look into SEO Help

Chapter 6: First Staging Project Requested. What Do I Do???!!!

It has been a fun journey so far and you are starting to see all the parts of the business come together. Your business is set up with the state, admin items are done and prepped, you know your price structures, website is up and running, first marketing meetup completed. You get a call from a realtor you met at the meetup last week and they are requesting your help. Woohoo! Now it's time to get this baby in motion, but what do you do? Where do you start? How do you reply to your first client?

This can be very exciting and you could possibly get so overwhelmed you say the wrong things. Whatever you do, stay calm and ask the right questions. Don't over promise and tell them you can stage the property tomorrow! Think before you speak. I got you. Follow along as I help prepare you on how to chat with your client, get the right info to start the process, prep for the job, and finish successfully!

The First Conversation

- **What is the projected list date for the market and property address?**
    - Always start by asking the client when they are trying to have the home listed on the market and go "live". Then work backwards. Most realtors want to be live and have the property on MLS (multiple listing service) on

either a Thursday evening or Friday. With that said, ideally, we try to stage the property for them on the Monday, Tuesday, or Wednesday morning/afternoon before the list date. This allows them ample time to have a photographer come in and take pictures, edit, and post the listing.

- o Make sure you have your calendar ready and open when talking with the clients so you are not overbooking yourself as well as giving yourself enough time to prepare for the stage.
- o Always find out the property address to make sure it is in your desired location area. I messed this up one day and booked a stage 2 hours away not even thinking about the extra trip charge and time it would take to even get there before staging. Let's just say, I barely made money on this job and then spent too much time driving!

- **Is the property going to be occupied or vacant during the listing?**
  - o It is important to know what your client needs. They might need advice on how to set up the home with current furnishings or they might need you to bring in inventory. This will also determine the schedule too. Most occupied consults can be done at any time and several weeks to months before the list date. When you have to bring in inventory, you need to work with the list date.
  - o **Occupied consult only**-If the client needs advice on current furniture and accessories,

explain to them your process (walk through then provide a report), and what it costs.

- **Occupied staging-**This again is where the seller's will be living in the home during the listing. If you decide to go this way and offer this service, explain your process and give projected costs (sometimes these are difficult to give until you go preview the home). Make sure you are also clear with your client about your policies when bringing in your inventory to someone's home while they are living there. These policies should be different than a vacant stage because of damage, use, pets, etc. and have more costs because of the liability. Never assume the clients know anything about this. The more upfront you are before you even get started the better.

- **Vacant staging-**If the property will be vacant, find out when the home will be completely vacant and cleaned. This will also give you more intel on scheduling details. Provide your starting cost for staging. Explain your process. Give an example of what types of furniture and items you include in your staging.

- **Side note:** Since this is your first job, you of course want to say "Yes" to everything. Totally fine and dandy, just be open minded and pay attention to how things play out. We used to take everything, no matter how big or small. No matter if sellers were living in the home with our inventory or if they had pets, etc. In a way, that was good for us. It showed

- **When can you preview the home?**
    - Once you have determined what the client needs in terms of staging, then ask when you are able to either preview the home or set up a consultation. Sometimes it is helpful to know if you are meeting clients at the home or doing the walk through by yourself. This is most helpful when you have a busy schedule. If I am meeting with clients, I always make sure I am dressed nice and appropriate. If I am doing the walk through by myself, then I have more flexibility. Always show up professional when you can!

Time to Preview the Home (Occupied Staging or Vacant Staging)

Sometimes, you will preview the home with the realtor or the seller. Other times, you are there alone. Either way, there are several things you need to do while walking the property.

- **Take pictures:** Before you pull out the camera, be sure to ask if it is ok to take pictures of the home so you are being respectful of the sellers' property. Never assume it is ok to snap away without asking. When taking photos, always get pictures of the main rooms, kitchen, bathrooms. When starting out, take pictures of all spaces, even the back patio or front porch. This way, when you are working on laying out the inventory and what you need, you can refer back to the photos. I typically only go to a home once before we actually stage it, so I can only reference photos while preparing for the stage.

- **Analyze the home:** Pay attention to wall textures, location of outlets, doorway or door frame sizes, access into the home, flooring materials, bathroom towel bar/rings, window locations, size of rooms. Take your time, especially in the beginning, to focus on the details of the home. *Measure, measure, measure.* There were several instances where I did not measure the width of a doorframe and brought in a sucker of a sofa that would not fit through the front door or the back door. Idiot. We not only damaged our sofa, but I had to pay for touch ups on the trim of the door we damaged as well. So always look at those details. *Measure the room*s too so you know what size sofa or loveseat or dining table or bed to bring in. Also pay attention to the *wall texture*. We work in a lot of older homes that have plaster walls. Nails do not like to go into these walls, so we had to come up with other solutions in order to hang art. Know where the *outlets* are for lamps. We have learned over the years to always bring extension cords because outlets can be in weird spots. Pay attention to the *flooring*. Do you need a rug? If so, what size? Look at the *hardware* in the bathrooms. How many towels do you need? What type of towels do you need? Analyze the *paint color* on the walls. Are they neutral? Is there a focal color that you need to incorporate in the design? The more you focus on and understand the layout of the home, the better you can service your clients. Also do not be afraid to ask questions!

- **Apartment building or condo-These are unique and can take more time and money:** Just keep that in mind. Questions to ask yourself: Do you have to take the stairs or elevator, etc. How large of an opening is the elevator? If it is a small elevator, what size furniture will fit? If stairs are involved, will the job take longer and cost more than a normal job? If you are staging a condo/high rise, pay attention to access into the building. Always talk with the building manager at the front desk. Many times, you will have to provide paperwork, insurance for your truck divers, a deposit fee, and non-refundable fees for elevator use. If this is the case, add that into your costs. You will also have to request certain times and dates for blocking out the elevators. Be sure to get the phone number and paperwork info before you leave the building!

- **Next day photography:** In the beginning, I highly advise letting your clients know that you need to have the flexibility to stage a home and request that photos be done the day after you stage. The reason why, you might need to hire a moving company to do the heavy lifting and sometimes their schedules push you to stage the home in the afternoon or morning. You will not know until you call to reserve. This is important to be transparent with your clients up front that you aren't exactly sure of the timeframe until the project is confirmed and contracted. Once you do this more often and work with hired movers, you can make a better judgment of when photos can be taken after you stage.

- **Ask questions and understand expectations:** Now that you have gone to the home and processed what you saw or still at the home with the realtor or seller, get even more answers. Do they plan on leaving the home the way it is for selling? Are they painting any walls, changing flooring or materials in the home? Do they have a preference of what rooms they want staged? Do they like a muted palette of color or want pops of color? Do they prefer lots of accessories or like a minimal vibe? Do they have an overall idea of what they see as a design in the home? Always be confident in yourself that you have the design eye and style but it is important to understand the client's expectations. This could also warrant a higher cost in staging, so be mindful. I have run into some clients in the past, who had very high expectations and wanted a luxury vibe but I didn't ask the right questions in the beginning and we ran into a big issue come stage day. They weren't happy and I couldn't provide what they wanted, so we had to remove the staging. Yes, I lost money. Yes, this was on me. As a business owner, if you want to be successful, never over promise and assume anything. Always ask, even if you feel they are dumb questions. But if you do not understand what your client expects (especially if they are new to you), then you will not have happy repeat clients. And if their expectations are way over what you can provide, then happily decline the job. There is no shame in saying you are not the right fit for them. Find your style and niche, be proud, and don't look back.

Send Proposal and Ask for the Sale

Now that you have done your due diligence and asked all the questions and feel great about the job in front of you, time to write up that proposal and send it.

- **Write the proposal:** You should have already set up your template to send out the proposal to your clients. From here, add in the person's info and property address. Include the rooms that will be staged. As well as a brief description of what will be included. For example, If we are staging the living room, I will include on the proposal:

Furniture rental for living room includes sofa, 1-2 chairs, rug, coffee table, end tables, possible console table, art, accessories

I keep it somewhat vague on the proposal because sometimes, when in the middle of staging, I might decide 2 chairs will clutter the space. It's ok to give yourself some flexibility when staging.

- **Be upfront and transparent about cost:** On the proposal, make sure the sellers and realtors understand the full extent to your cost. For example, we charge one flat fee lumped together that includes the initial consult/walk through, staging prep, delivery, and removal for our minimum staging. I make sure that is written out on the proposal so all parties are on the same page. If they want more than three rooms staged, I will add additional lines on the proposal with costs next to each space to show them the extra charges. I also add a line at the bottom to provide them with additional costs for extension past one month. If they need another month of staging, it costs "x" amount of dollars. It is so important to be transparent, especially in the beginning of your business venture, so you can gain trust and repeat clients. You do not have to break down every little cost for them. You are just giving them the full picture so they do not have hidden fees later on.

- **Include a separate line item for deposit charge:** In the beginning, this will be very important for you to be upfront with your clients about a deposit. This deposit will be your life line on starting out purchasing the furniture. You need to require a deposit fee so you have the capability of staging a home for them. The deposit charge is typically half of the first month's rental cost. That amount will allow you to purchase the inventory items and pay for a moving truck, etc to begin the stage. By adding this to the proposal, you are again being transparent to your clients and gaining their trust.

- **Ask for the sale:** Once you emailed the proposal to the client, be sure to follow up with them and ask if they have any further questions and would like to proceed with the staging. Always ask for the sale. I worked retail for years and the most important thing was to ask, follow through with the purchase. Most clients are waiting on you to make the first step. After you ask for the sale, and they say yes, move forward with your contract.

Send Contract and Get Deposit

You have the first "Yes"! Yay, now the logistics. You should have your contract prepped and ready from the beginning stages of starting the business, now it's time to fill in the spaces.

- **What to additionally include in the contract besides the legality portion:**
    - Be sure to include the person's name in the contract, who will be responsible for the payment and liabilities on the rental furniture at the property.
    - Include the staging address.

- o   Include the time frame -start date of delivery to end date of the first 30 days of rental.
- o   Include the cost for extending another month.
- o   Include space for the billing information to be added by the person signing the contract.
- o   Include space for date signed.
- o   Includes space for signature.
- **Get the Deposit:** Clients have signed the contract and returned it to you. Now grab that deposit so you can get moving with the process. This also shows how committed they are to moving forward with the staging.
- **Get instructions on how to access the property for the delivery of staging:** Always ask how you will access the property when you deliver the furniture. Most times, you are given a lockbox number. Sometimes the realtor or seller will meet you there to let you know. Just be sure you know beforehand so you are not paying extra for mover's time (if applicable) waiting to be let in to do your job! **Side note: Typically the lockbox code is given a few days before to you. I always make a note in my calendar to reach out to the client a few days before so I am prepared for the day of staging. I will also add the lockbox code in my calendar with the delivery address so they are both together and so I don't lose it!

Confirm with Movers

This portion might not pertain to you if you have your own vehicle to move the furniture into the home. However, if you need to rent a moving truck, it is now time to get on their schedule. If you are going to use a moving company to do the heavy lifting, be sure to ask their time frame of when they would show up to the first address where the inventory is stored. You also should have found a few options for moving companies before getting to this point so you are ready to rock n roll. But if not, be sure to ask these moving companies all the questions listed in the "research" chapter. If you are renting a truck or movers, you will typically pay upfront for this cost. Again this cost can range from $250-$500 per move.

Total Cost: Up to $500 depending on moving company

Buy and Prep Inventory

Now the fun part! Backtrack to your proposal and look at the pieces of furniture you included for each room so you are certain you do not forget anything. This is your starting point for what to buy and to be certain you have everything you need for the day of staging. This is a crucial step to be successful in your business. I have always been one to stay organized and prepared even as a child but now, it is vital for this business's success. Always be prepared. Remember that we have now spent up to $1,015 on startup costs plus moving costs up to $500. This gives you a remaining $985 or so to spend on furniture and inventory PLUS your deposit from your client. That deposit will vary depending on what you are charging your client for the first month of staging. For example, you charge $2000 for the first month of staging, so your deposit will be $1000. That will give you $1985 for the remainder of the spending. It is very doable to purchase all items with about $1500, especially if you "shopped" your home at first! Follow along as I guide you through how to get prepped.

- **Create the list:** Start by listing off the big pieces: sofa, dining table, chairs, coffee table, bed, etc. Then focus on the smaller items. It might help if you breakdown each room on the list too so you know for sure you are not missing a thing. See below as an example for a room.
  - Living Room-
    - Sofa (light colored/no more than 84" long)
    - 2 chairs (small scale-going on small wall)
    - Coffee table (round will work best)
    - 2 end tables (on a small side, maybe square)
    - 1 console table (around 48" long)
    - 1 (5 x 8 rug)
    - 2 lamps (1 table lamp, 1 floor lamp)
    - 4-5 pillows and 1 blanket for the upholstery

- 4 pieces of art (1 mirror-maybe black frame, 1 large piece over the console table, 2 smaller pieces on the small wall)
- 6-8 books for the table tops
- 4 plants
- 4-5 vases/decor items

I like to include descriptions of some of the items so when I am looking for these pieces I remember what will work best in the home. Do this type of detailed list for each space you are staging. I know once you finish it will seem so overwhelming and your eyes are probably seeing dollar signs, but I have some tricks for you to make it happen in your budget (and no you are not robbing a home goods store!)

- **Shop your home:** For the first few stages, I saved a lot of money using some of my own decor, art, lamps, and small furniture. My family was totally onboard not having a few end tables and barstools for a month or so. Thank goodness! I only "shopped" my home using items that were in good condition. I did not want to bring in a damaged piece especially on my first stage. It is so important to start with a good impression. I used my own hardback books and took off the covers. I used a few vases and candles. I took some of my neutral art off the walls. I had some end tables in the guest bedroom that worked perfectly on the first stage. The funny thing about all this, I decluttered some of my home and ended up keeping it that way and donated the items to my staging inventory!

****Total Cost: FREE*

- **Shop thrift stores/online local groups/garage sales:** Once I shopped at my home, I next went to the local thrift stores in the area and took a look to see what they had. I tried to hone in on good/great condition items and items that I think would enhance the home, not hinder. I looked at art, lamps, small furniture items, barstools, dining chairs, and decor. I found a few things that I knew I could spray paint to look more modern and cleaned up so I was able to save quite a bit that way. Always feel open minded going into these stores. By rolling up your sleeves and doing the hard work, you can save lots of money, especially in the beginning. **Side note: A secret of mine. I shop for books at the dollar stores because you can find great deals and cheap books since you just need them as props! Always go for the hardback books. You can also check out the local online groups that sell furniture and items in your area. This is great because you can find inexpensive sofas and dining sets on here and save quite a bit! Try to find the majority of your items in thrift stores, garage sales, and online marketplaces. It is amazing what you can get and get quickly for very low prices. I have found two sets of nice looking chairs for $100 in an online marketplace and a great sofa for $250. Normally these costs would be double if bought new. SAVE SAVE SAVE your first few stages.

- **Buy the remaining items:** Now that you have exhausted all the thrift shops in your area and bought a few things from the online groups, it's time to finalize your list and see what else you need. Depending on time, you could buy online through some of the online furniture companies like Wayfair or even Amazon. You could also shop at TJ Maxx or Marshalls for inexpensive items. Just keep in mind that you are spending wisely so you still have money to pay your movers if need be.

Total Cost: Up to $1500 of your remaining costs

- **Wrap items:** You have all of your items bought and stored in your garage, etc. Now time to wrap. I wish I started this prep in the very beginning. I did not realize how dirty moving trucks can be and how dirty your hands can get when moving all these things. We had to get rid of a lot of furniture in the first year or so because of getting damaged while moving the items too. So, get some 15"-18" long plastic wrap rolls (you can find them online or in the big department stores) and wrap all furniture and art. These can run around $50-$100. I found a 4 pack on Amazon for about $60 and have them delivered once a month to always have on hand. Get in this habit to project your inventory and extend the life of your investments.

Total Cost: Up to $100 for 4-8 rolls

- **Prep a "Go" bag:** Lastly, get yourself a bag of goodies. This bag should go on every stage delivery and stage removal. It should have several important items inside. The longer you do this business, the more you can cater to your own needs of what to bring to each stage. You would be surprised what items you have below. Keep your costs minimal but if you need to purchase everything, you are looking around $100. See my go-to list below.

    o   Hammer and finish nails

    o   Screwdrivers (Flathead and Phillips)

    o   Microfiber towels for cleaning

- Glass cleaner for mirrors and glass tops
- Wood markers with a variety of colors for marking up damaged areas on the wood
- A few extension cords
- Scissors
- Super glue
- Wood glue
- Light bulbs (pack of 4)
- Allen wrench set (to help tighten bolts)
- Toilet paper (you never know if you have to go!)

Total Cost: Up to $100

- **Create a quick floor plan guide:** In the beginning, it is very helpful to draw out a quick floor plan of how you will layout the big furniture pieces. I like to draw a quick sketch of each room and position the furniture layout as best as I can. This helps me prep my design layout and saves me lots of time when actually staging the home. It will also give you some confidence and ease in order to give direction to the movers on where to place the items. Over time, you can easily do this in your head before getting to the home.

- **Snag some plastic storage bins:** I learned quickly that it is a pain in the butt to not have my accessories (books, fake plants, decor, towels, etc) organized in storage bins. We did purchase 3-4 bins in the beginning but it was totally worth it. I am able to move them more easily and efficiently in the bins. You could probably find some online or at thrift shops at a decent price. Or use some of your own to save lots of money! If you need to buy new, you can easily find 18 gallon storage tubs for around $7-8 a piece. You only need 3-4 storage bins for each home!

Total Cost: Up to $32 plus tax

Stage Day

It's here! The first big day. Get ready to roll up your sleeves and create a masterpiece!

- **Get out your list:** Make sure you double and triple check your list of items that you need and have ready to be loaded into the truck. It is important to not forget items and make silly mistakes. You do not want to have to go back to the home multiple times because you forgot something.

- **Make sure you have your go bag: You** will need this to hang art, clean up, and mark any damaged furniture if need be.

- **Confirm the lockbox code for access into the home:** This is a must so you can actually get into the home and do your job!

- **Confirm time for the mover's arrival:** Add this to your to do list if this is part of your plan.

- **Start with the rugs:** Once at the home, start unloading. I like to start with rugs first if need be. If you have a large rug that the sofa or dining table needs to go on top of, get those in place first. It makes it a lot easier to adjust later.

- **Bring in the big items:** Have the movers place the large furniture in the correct place. This would be the time to make adjustments with the larger pieces. If you put the sofa on the wrong wall, have the movers move it now. It makes it easier too since you do not have much else in the space. Then continue with the smaller items.

- **Bring in the bins, lamps, pillows, and art:** I always ask my movers to place my accessories bins and art in a good spot so that I can easily access all the items without it being in the way of other things. I like to take out all the accessories and place them on the kitchen counters so I can see what I have and make quick decisions about where to place them.

- **Decorate:** Take a moment to decide how you want to start. I like to stage room by room so I can focus on each space individually. You do what is best for you. Hang the art, plug in the lamps. Add the accessories. Step back and make sure you are happy with the end result. Not going to lie, we move our accessories around multiple times in each space. It is ok to do so! Make the design how you want it. Your name is on the ticket.

- **Walk through/Finish up:** Once you have all rooms staged and to your liking, go back through each space making sure everything looks good. This is the time that we go back and clean the glass tops, dust off the tables, mark up the wood furniture that has scratches, etc. Also do a final walkthrough before you leave.

- **Take pictures:** Be proud! You just finished your first stage! Yay! Make it a memory by taking pictures. I highly suggest taking a few pictures of each space. These will not only help you remember what you placed in the home, but this will be a way to capture your work and use it on your social media platforms, website, and marketing materials. If you can, take close ups. Take pictures of several rooms in one shot. I like to make sure all lights are on and window coverings are up. I like to also make sure I do not have weird things like trash cans or cars from outside windows in my photos too. Might have to adjust your angle in the room.

- **Get the final payment:** Once done, I like to send a few photos of the house to my client and ask for the final payment at the same time. I am sure you are feeling a little nervous with all the spending upfront but now you will receive the other half of the payment and should feel at ease knowing this will help continue the growth.

Ask For Reviews, Referrals, Feedback

This step is crucial to do right after the job has been completed. While the clients are raving about the great job you did, be sure to ask for a review, a referral, and feedback.

- **Reviews:** Always, always ask your clients for a quick review. Our business growth has been word of mouth. The review and remarks from past clients have brought us so much work because there is trust and validation and confidence from peers that by using us, they will be taken care of. If you do not have your business set up on Google yet, get the clients to send you a few quick words via text or email about the work you did. Ask them if they would be ok if you share this on your social media. It is vital to have word of mouth on how you did. The more prospective clients can see reviews about your business, the more growth you will receive. If you have set up your business through Google (very simple and free), you can actually email or text your clients a Google review link from Google which will upload online so clients can see the reviews when they find you on Google. There is hardly anything you have to do for this but just send them the link. This is very helpful for new clients who are not familiar with you at all and find you searching for help in your area.

- **Referral:** This is an important step to follow through on so you can get more work. Along with asking the client for a review right after the job is complete, ask for a referral. Most realtors have lots of realtor friends. Do not be shy of asking. Referrals are free marketing tools and we know free is fabulous!

- **Feedback:** The last thing you want to ask your client is how you did for them? Can they offer any feedback on what you can do better next time or what they really liked about your service this time? Feedback is great. It can reassure you that you are doing a great job. It can also humble you and give you guidance on how to make things even better. Do not take bad feedback as a negative. Always look at it as a way to grow. There were many times over the years that I had to walk away with my tail between my legs but man did it give me a different perspective and push me to grow and be a better business owner and better person. Any feedback is good feedback. Always stay open minded.

- **Celebrate:** Gosh darn it, you just completed your first gig. Celebrate. Never forget to take a step back and be proud of what you did. High five your friends and family. Do a happy dance. Whatever the case maybe, enjoy and be proud.

****GRAND TOTAL FOR ALL ITEMS: Up to $2,232*

Now that you have finished up the first stage of the business, let's see the overall breakdown on the costs spent. This will show you that you definitely can make this happen with $2500!!

Starting Investment:

    $2,500

    <u>-$ 690 Startup Costs Including Registration</u>

    $1,810 Remaining

    <u>$ 70 Website/Domain Costs</u>

    $1,740 Remaining

    <u>$ 255 Marketing Material Costs</u>

    $1,485 Remaining

    <u>-$500 Moving Costs To Deliver to the Home</u>

    $985 Remaining

Initial Deposit from 1st Stage:

    $800 (as an example/50% down)

  -$1,500 Furniture and Accessories

  <u>-$232 For Furniture Wrap and "Go" Bag Items</u>

    $53 Remaining

Final Deposit from 1st Stage:
<u>$800 (50% remaining for the first month of stage)</u>

    $853 Left Over!!!

**These prices are subject to change.

See it is possible! It is wonderful to have money left over so you can keep moving forward! I highly suggest saving at least $500 to use for the removal of the furniture at the first stage because at some point you will need to hire movers to get it out when the home is sold. Make mental notes of this so you do not forget! Use the remaining money for the next stage!

Chapter 6 Recap: Use this checklist to make sure you cover each section before moving on!

- Ask Questions About the Property
- Preview the Property
- Send the Proposal/Ask for the Sale
- Create the Contract/Get Signed
- Ask for Initial Deposit
- Set Time with Movers
- Create a List of Inventory Items
- Buy Inventory Items -Shop Home First!
- Stage the Home
- Asks for Reviews and Referrals

Chapter 7: Get Ready, Get Set, GOALS!

You are a few months into the business and have had the chance to help multiple clients with their properties and you are starting to get the hang of it. You have quickly learned how to work with clients and how to be successful on each project. The next important part of becoming a successful business is to create goals to continue growing and moving forward. I can't tell you how important it was for us to make monthly goals, quarterly goals, annual goals, five year goals, and even ten year goals for our company. This gave us drive, direction, and a way to check-in and make sure we were on the path we wanted to create for our business. It is important to make two types of goals for your business: small, quick obtainable goals and long term goals. It is also important to understand how to create a goal for your business. I will break it down for you!

How to create a goal

You would think this step would be easy. Not always. Goal setting can come natural to some but then others, it is like pulling teeth. I found this out quite easily when I was teaching elementary school students for a few years. Some kiddos totally could nail setting up goals for themselves and others really needed some time and guidance. If you are one of those who just needs step by step, line by line help, I got you! If you can create goals in your sleep, move on to the next section or hell, take a minute and review how to make them just to be on the safe side. No matter how excelled you are in goal setting, don't forget to WRITE THEM DOWN!! Have your goals written down somewhere so you can physically see the goals. Mental goals don't count. What if you came up with the most fantastic goal in your head and you were super stoked to get started on it but you forgot to write it down and totally missed a key part. Don't do that to yourself. Write them down. Put them somewhere safe so you can always go back to them. Ok, off my rant, let's get started.

- **What do you want to accomplish?** It is important to start with something you want to see happen in your business. What do you want to accomplish? What do you want more of? Do you want to stage more homes next month? Do you want to gain more clients? Do you want to profit more money each month? Begin with the most pressing thing on your mind. I always take the route of making one of our goals to increase the amount of homes we stage each month to each year. That has always been my first intention. You have to start somewhere. Your business plan and growth could be different from ours so do what is best for your model. I like to have three to five goals/accomplishments set for each month and each year. Jot down at least three things you want to grow in your business. It does not have to be specific at first, just get the idea down. For example, "I want to stage more homes next month". Then you can add to each goal in more depth.

- **How will you measure it?** Great! You have your three ideas written down. That is a wonderful start. Now, let's get more detailed. To be successful, you must make your goals more detailed and focused so you can measure the growth. Adding a measurement to your goals will also help you project the income, profits, and expenses for the following years of your business. It will guide you on where you are going. It is a very important detail to add to your goal setting. Let's keep with the example from the last step, "I want to stage more homes next month." Okay, how many. Let's say you staged 3 homes last month. You felt it was somewhat hard for you to gain the momentum to obtain all three stages. You think you could possibly stage 5 homes this month with a little extra push into marketing yourself to more realtors. So let's make it a goal. "I want to stage 5 homes this month." By giving it a measurable amount, you have a number to try to meet and can push yourself to accomplish. By also adding a measurable amount, you are able to calculate how many more stages you could do the rest of the year and so forth for your future.

- **Can it really be done?** In the previous step, you decided you want to aim for 5 homes to be staged. This last month, you did 3. It was a little difficult to get all three clients but one of the realtors mentioned they would give your name to their office. This could give you the opportunity to build more clientele. If you use this resource given to you and meet up with some of the realtors, then you might believe 5 homes is attainable. You also might believe that the other two clients from the past month would be great referrals for your future clients and you know you can ask them for more potential work. This will also help make 5 homes achievable this coming month. You feel confident that goal can be reached. An unattainable goal might be going from 3 homes to 15 homes in one month. BUT, if you can prove that it is attainable and have the means to make it happen, then by golly, go for it!

- **Give yourself an end date.** This you would think would be an easy addition to your goal but some will completely forget to add it in. Always give yourself an end date to a goal. If you have no end date, you have no pressure or drive to get it done in a timely manner. You could say, " I want to stage 5 homes." Ok cool, like next week, in a day, in a year, in your lifetime? Give it a firm end date. So the goal we set in the previous sections is great, "I want to stage 5 homes this month." That gives a set time to make it happen. If it doesn't happen in that time frame, then you are able to reassess and start again with a more achievable goal in the time you want.

- **How can you make it achievable?** You have your goal written down. You know the measurement set. You know the timeframe set. Now can you make it achievable? What steps can you take to get this goal met? These steps do not have to be written down formally but just listed underneath your goal so you are able to see what you need to do to make it happen. We know that the realtor you just worked with gave your name to their office. So, let's add a line item underneath your goal that you will reach out to the realtor office and see if you can meet with the other realtors, bring them some breakfast, and hand out some marketing materials. You could also list out that you will ask the other two clients for one referral if they are able to help. Those are ways to know you can meet your goal. By including the steps you need to take to hit the goal in your goal setting process, you are already a step ahead to making it all happen.

Always Think Bigger Picture

Now, I am very aware that smaller goals feel more attainable and I make many smaller goals throughout the year. BUT, as an entrepreneur, it is so important to not think small. You must try to see the bigger picture. If you want your business to thrive, you need to look forward so you can see where the business can go and grow. How do you see the business evolve and expand? Do you see yourself in the same spot in five years, ten years? Taking a moment to really think about the future of the business is so important. This allows you to truly foresee where you want to go with all this. Is this just a fun hobby to make some extra cash on the side or do you want to grow the business or even take it global. You have to decide your direction. Every business venture will have a different agenda and this is a great time to define where you want to go. Look at the overall picture. Once you do that, then you can pull the layers back and break down the big goals into smaller goals/pieces week by week, month by month, year by year. This is how the small attainable goals become part of the bigger picture and you are able to see progression.

- **Make the "BIG" goal.** This goal, future outlook, for your business is a starting point for you. It is ok to not know exactly where you want to go with your business but it is important to start thinking about it. My first year's focus was just to start making a profit and build relationships. I was new at this business thing and wanted to just keep my head above water. I wish I had someone who could have given me insight on thinking bigger and continue to look forward. If you don't have any mentors or influencers in your life yet, I am here to help you!

Let's look at a few examples of "Big" goals. Maybe this will help you get the ball rolling and create a target to aim for. If not, it's ok. Your goals have to relate to your values.

- I will gross a million dollars annually within ten years of opening the business.

- I will have a large warehouse and storefront to meet clients within ten years.

- I will have five locations across the country within ten years .

- I will have employees/managers run the business for me so I can step back within ten years.

Let's walk through one of these examples together so you can see how to take a large intention and then begin to break it down step by step.

"I want to gross a million dollars annually within ten years." At first as a business, we discussed where we see ourselves in ten years and we definitely went big. My excited and enthusiastic mind was ready to rock the world (ok Denver) and push beyond our boundaries. We started here. It is totally fine to dream big. If not, then what's the point of the process and drive?! I did, however, do the math. When you break that down in an annual goal, that averages about 42 homes a month to stage and totals 500 homes a year. Yes a business can obtain that, but did I want to make that happen. That would mean a lot of furniture and a huge cost for a warehouse to store all that furniture. So instead, we backtracked a little and brought the "Big" goal down to: *I want to gross half a million dollars annually within ten years.* This brought the monthly staging amount down to about 20 homes a month and

240 homes a year. Way more attainable but still allowing us to look ahead at the bigger picture of the business. We had to look at our values and how we wanted the business to grow. Our focus was to grow the business organically and be the "turtle" in the race. Slow and steady was our pace. By setting this "Big" goal we are always able to have forward motion and a way to gauge where we are in the process. In the next section, we will continue with this "Big" goal and break it down into smaller goals to make it more obtainable.

Break it down

You now have an overall intention for your business. How do you accomplish this? Where do you even start? Let's break it down into more simple steps and goals so you can feel as if you can obtain your "Big" goal a lot easier. By starting small and setting shorter term goals, you are able to accomplish things quickly and create more confidence in yourself to help push through the harder and longer term goals.

- **Five/Ten year goals.** These goals could also be analyzed as large goals and I would agree with that. If your "Big" goal is set as a ten year goal, then your next step would be to make a five year goal. This can be a quick and easy thing to create. Let's go back to the "Big" goal example: *I want to gross half a million dollars annually within ten years.* Ok so if I calculated that I need to stage 240 homes a year to make that much gross income by year ten, then by year five, I would hope to be on track for staging 120 homes a year. I am literally cutting the "Big" goal in half. **Side note: This does not account for price increases throughout the years. It is essential to increase your prices over time in relation to inflation, competition, etc. This goal still seems attainable for year five of the business and helps steer me to stay on track through the first five years of growth. This type of goal is really providing a path for me to follow. I am working backwards to move forward. Not every business owner is going to break down all their goals in this format and that's ok. This process helped me see where I needed to be annually to continue to make headway and aim for my overall goal for the future of the business.

- **Yearly goals.** My annual goals are slightly different every year and I also add more to my plate to push myself each year. These goals are like making "New Year's Resolutions" even though I never make those because "Annual Goals" actually get met. Each December, I print out my P&L report for the year (Profit and Loss Report) and see how we did. We base our next year's goals on increasing profits, projects, etc by 15%-30%. This is a healthy increase each year and has really kept us on our target goal for our ten year mark. We might add two or three new goals for ourselves but always go back to our "Big" goal too and make sure we are on track with that one as well. So going back to the "Big" goal, if we need to be staging around 240 homes a year by year ten with a 15%-30% increase each year, I need to find out what my aim is per year. Give yourself some grace here. Some years are amazing at growth and some years, you might stay stagnant. Just stay positive and remember why you started the business.

- **Monthly goals.** These goals stay simple for our business. These usually go hand and hand with the yearly goals that are really just broken down into 12 months. I look at these as smaller/more achievable goals for the bigger picture of the year. I also take into account that the holiday months, November and December are usually slower. July is also slower because of summer vacations and the last hoorah before school starts. With this said, I might give these months smaller goals compared to the Spring when it is crazy busy. I will bulk up the achievements for these months. I will set the monthly goals and look at them once a week to make sure I am on track. If we are off or short, I will have a quick meeting with my business partner on how we can make the goals attainable for the month. Maybe marketing comes into play. Maybe I will send a few emails to our regular clients to see how their schedules are shaping up and if there is anything we can help with. This might generate some work or at least add work to another month if they have a home coming up on the market in the future.

- **Weekly goals.** Maybe I am a little "Cray Cray" to set weekly goals for myself but man does it help give me direction for each week. There are times I feel like I have hit a brick wall and not sure which way is up. However, when I get stuck, I always refer back to weekly intentions and goals. Setting weekly goals can help steer you in the right direction and keep you on the path to meeting and exceeding your goals.

Try, Try, Again

There are going to be many goals you do not reach or accomplish. IT IS OK! Over the years I have gone through ups and downs and there would be weeks or even months I would not reach my goals. I might have a little issue with perfectionism but being a business owner, I have humbled myself over and over and have learned to roll with the punches and let things go. With that said, I never give up on myself and always reflect on what goals I do not achieve. Instead of criticizing myself, I learn how to readjust the goal based on what obstacles I face and try again.

Do not ever give up on yourself. You must be your biggest cheerleader and have to give yourself grace. Owning a business and creating a successful business takes patience, time, energy, and motivation. Keep going. Reflection is super important and it is ok to aim for the same goal again. It's the action that you take the second time that makes the difference. If you can, find a mentor or friend or family member that owns a business to help give you some guidance on how to set yourself up for success. What did they do when they missed a goal or how do they approach goal setting for themselves? Community is everything and never be afraid to ask for help!!

Chapter 7 Recap: Use this checklist to make sure you cover each section before moving on!

- Create Goals for the Business that can be Attainable
- Create an Overall Goal for the business-The "Big" Goal
- Create Annual Goals
- Create Monthly Goals
- Create Weekly Goals
- Try, Try, Again

Chapter 8: Maintain and Thrive.

Congratulations on getting through the hard stuff and getting your business going! You should be proud of yourself and excited on this amazing journey. It is so important to recognize how far you have come through this process and to continue to maintain the drive and effort. There are several things I suggest you follow through on to keep up the growth and success of the business. Definitely create a system that works for you to manage all your jobs, inventory, invoices, money, etc. Maintain a running "to-do" list because so many things pop up when operating a business. It can get overwhelming really quickly! Continue to make goals for yourself. Find a community who can help you through the struggles and also celebrate all wins, big and small. Don't just coast through. Lastly, always keep looking forward and continue to follow up with your clients.

Create A System

In order to stay organized and on top of your jobs, goals, schedule, etc. you must create a system that works for you. What does this mean? Put in place ways to keep track of everything you do, so you can always stay on top of what is going on in the business and not forget simple things or big things. In order to maintain and thrive, staying organized is the best thing any business owner can do! The big things that I focus on are our staging jobs and inventory. See how I do it.

- Job Schedule: I have two ways of keeping track of my job schedule. I use the calendar on my phone to let me know when a job is going and I created a spreadsheet to show me when each job starts and is up for the month. On my calendar, I add the address, lockbox, and time when we will stage the job. This is great for me because when I am trying to schedule other jobs with clients or consults, I can easily pull my phone out and figure out what days and times I have available for the next stage. For my spreadsheet, I use Google Sheets to set up the schedule of all my stages throughout the year in one place. It is fabulous because every year I add a new sheet so I can easily go back to the previous years and compare my growth. On the sheet I include several bits of info for each job to help me.
  - The name of the realtor/seller.
  - The address of the stage.
  - The cost of what I charged the client for the first month.
  - The date of install.
  - The date of removal.
  - If the stage is vacant or partial.
  - If the stage went into another month.
  - The cost of the second month.
  - If the stage went under contract (yes or no).
  - The cost of the property when listed.
  - The cost of the property when sold.

All this info helps keep me on track and reminds me to follow up with the clients if we need to pull the furniture or extend. I like the Google Sheets because I can easily change the date of extension/removal or highlight properties that need attention. It has also been a great way to see growth through the years and make projections for monthly stages based on the previous year.

- <u>Inventory</u>: Once you have accumulated a lot of inventory over the years, it can get very overwhelming to keep track of what you have. I again used Google Sheets to help create a basic way of knowing what is in our warehouse and what is staged in homes. Do I track everything? No. I just track sofas, loveseats, dining tables, end tables, coffee tables, console tables, bookcases, accent chairs, rugs, art, lamps, beds, bedding, large tree plants, and outdoor furniture sets. I do not keep up with pillows, blankets, or table top accessories. I would be tracking inventory 24 hours a day if I did that. My business partner and I came up with a plan of what would be the most important pieces to track so we can at least see if we have enough furniture to cover a new property or to see where certain items are located. Now, this process took some time to get going. I did not set this up right away and I wish I would have! It took hours to create. I suggest getting it started the moment you buy furniture. Then every time you buy something else, take a few moments to add to the list that day so you never miss a beat! This setup works for us and is easily maintainable. You will need to create a system that works for you! When I created this list, I broke out sections of the items. For example, I have a section for sofas, loveseats, chairs, dining tables, coffee tables, end tables, console tables, beds, rugs, art, lamps, outdoor furniture, and tall plants. See below what items I include on our inventory sheet per each section.

- A picture of the furniture item.
- A quick description of the item.
- When it was purchased.
- The cost of the item.
- Where it is located (storage or a property address name ex. Clay Street).

All of this info is great for the business. Not only does it give me an idea of what we have and where it is currently located, it also allows me to see how much total cost of inventory (excluding accessories) we have at the bottom. I created a calculation so I can always see our total expenses. This also helps insurance too. If something was stolen, I have a clear documentation of what was in a certain home and the cost. I also have an overall total of what our inventory costs so all items are covered under insurance if there were a fire, etc.

Monthly Meetings

Another important part of our system we put in place is to have a monthly meeting to go over our growth, numbers, schedule, etc. We try to make this fun and meet for lunch and enjoy some bubbly over our P&L reports. These meetings keep us intune with how we are doing and if we need to adjust. I think communication is crucial, especially if you have a partner/s in the biz. When everyone is on the same page, the business can go way more smoothly. We discuss our upcoming schedule, our profits, our goals and how we are achieving them. We also keep up with our own personal schedules and see if we need to block out time for vacations or travel. Inventory is brought up too and if we need to add more to keep up with design trends or get rid of old items that are really damaged or outdated.

To-do Lists

In order to maintain sanity in my life, I have an ongoing to-do list for the biz. This has been extremely helpful for me to make sure I have an easy way to include all the things I need to take care of whether on the daily or weekly. I also find it very satisfying to check off a task and feel like I have accomplished things! You can go old school with your to-do lists and get a paper planner to hand write your to-do's or go paperless and use an app on your phone. I found that the program Asana has been a great asset for my check lists. They have a website or app that you can easily access on your phone. There are so many other programs out there to use and no matter what, organization is key!

I keep my to-do list limited to daily items and at the most weekly tasks. This way I am not overwhelming myself on too many things to take care of. I always look at my list in the morning before I get going for the day so I know my direction and order of what needs to be done. Prioritize your daily items, important things to be done first because at the end of the day, if I did not get to something, no big deal. I move that task to the next day. I have learned over the years not to sweat the small stuff because that can always be done another day. The beauty of apps and websites keeping track of your list is that you can quickly shift items to the next day or next week. Less time on mechanics and more time focusing on things that really matter.

Continue with Goals and Projections

Never stop creating goals for the biz! This is how you move forward, grow, and thrive! My business partner and I always create monthly goals and annual goals together. This helps motivate us to push ourselves and constantly improve. In our monthly meetings, we check back on the goals we made for the year and see where we need to focus our attention and celebrate when we meet our goals. We also check in with each other to make sure we are still on the right track for future projections and on the same page with our satisfaction with the business. By setting aside time to look at our goals during the monthly meetings, we are able to keep momentum and make sure the goals set will be attainable. This is also a great time to reassess and make new plans if need be.

It is vital to continue looking ahead for your business. Taking the time through the year to project, reflect, and adjust will not only benefit the growth of your business but it will help you stay motivated and excited about your successes.

Do Not Get Stagnant

This brings me to another important point, do not get stagnant! There are many ways this can happen in a business. If you aren't careful, you can get lazy on creating goals, staying on top of the trends, and continuing to market yourself to others. This can also hurt your business. Sometimes you can coast in your business and not have to work too hard to gain clients and jobs because the market is strong and keeps you busy. During this time, your mindset can run on autopilot. You might use the same furniture and same design themes over and over. Maybe set the same goals each quarter because they seem to work consistently for you. You might even forget to keep up with your current clients and make new ones. All of these issues can cause a stagnant point in your business and can actually be harmful to the growth of it over time.

What some won't tell you in the beginning of creating your staging business is that there are "feast" and "famine" times during the course of a business. What does this mean? It means that when things are hot, you are busy with clients, projects, jobs, etc. and do not have to work hard at all to keep up the momentum. These times are fabulous because your phone will be ringing off the hook for help. You are getting the chance to feast with profit and a busy schedule. On the opposite side of this "feasting" period, comes "famine". You are dead in the water. No jobs. The market is soft. Holidays are approaching. Big election year. Interest rates are up. Buyers are uncertain of what to do. This is when you must not stay stagnant and expect the work to come to you. You must do the work. Roll up your sleeves and get creative with your marketing techniques. Research current design trends to make sure you are on trend and desirable to your current clients and potential clients. Maybe it's time to buy new furniture or accessories to meet the high sought after trends. Continue to push yourself with goal setting so you are keeping the drive and spirit alive in the business. Always find ways to keep moving forward with your business. Yes, owning a business is hard work and seems like a 24/7 job. It is, BUT, those who stay excited and challenge themselves, will reap the rewards and enjoy the chaos of entrepreneurship.

Find A Community

Being a business owner can feel overwhelming and at times very difficult. It is ok to feel all these feelings. No matter how successful, business owners can feel deflated at times. That is just part of growing a business. To make these hard times as well as the good times better, find a community who can be a sounding board for you and support you in many ways.

I mentioned earlier in the researching section to look into realtor associations or home stager associations in your area. This can be huge for you to make friends in the same type of field as you. When you are struggling with any issues, go to this community. I am certain that they have run into the same problems before and can be a great avenue to get genuine advice. You could also find a business mentor (they do not have to be local or in the design field), to help you on your journey. A business mentor is someone who already has a successful business and can provide adequate details or tools to use to help navigate through struggles or hard times. They can also give support on how to maximize the great times. Do not feel alone. There are so many people who love to help and guide others. If I am asked by other stagers or realtors how to do something, I jump at the opportunity to share my wisdom. We are all in this together and there is so much abundance in this life for everyone. That's why there are communities out there for like minded individuals. Our human nature is to give and serve. Why not create a world where we can continue to help each other be successful and grow.

Thank Yous/Follow Ups

Thank you, thank you, thank you. These words are in my top five of highly used phrases. Being a business owner over the years, I have always made it a priority to stay humble and grateful. I still am one hundred percent. The absolute most important thing to do with your clients is to thank them for their continued support and be grateful for their added value to your business. After staging jobs are complete, we always reach back out and thank our realtors and sellers for using our services. We send quarterly and annual emails or texts to our main peeps and thank them again for their ongoing relationship with us. This is just another way to follow up with them so they know we are still here and think of them. If the budget allows, during the holidays, we send holiday cheer and gift cards to our clients to again show our gratitude and appreciation. I know this work might seem mundane and overkill but I feel in my heart this is just an easy way to share the love with my people and keep the spirit alive. This adds to our friendship and shows them we care and want to be of service. I personally feel you can't say "thank you" enough. That phrase will never push someone away.

Celebrate All Wins

The best way to finish up this chapter and book is to express how important it is to celebrate all wins for you and your business. It does not matter how big or small, celebrate any chance you get! Celebrations will continue to give you the joy, the drive, the energy, and any high vibes to keep you going and growing. If you just keep going from job to job, email to email, phone call to phone call, you will burn out hard and quickly. Your passion and love for the business will turn into anger, impatience, and regret. You will feel negative emotions and lose the reasoning of why you started this in the first place. Celebrate and be proud of everything you have accomplished in this endeavor.

There are so many ways to celebrate. These can be high fives to your colleagues. A coffee run for the team. Popping a bubbly after you stage your 1st home or even your 100th home. Lunch with your team to celebrate a great month of hard work. A Christmas bonus for exceeding all goals for the year. Find any and every way to celebrate and keep the joy alive. When you can step back and see the good, see the accomplishments, see how the long hours created great success, you will always be in alignment with your service to others. That's really the purpose of this business, to serve your community in the best light. So celebrate as often as you can!

Chapter 8 Recap: Use this checklist to make sure you cover each section before moving on!

- Create a System
- Have Monthly Meetings
- Create a Continued "To-Do" List
- Continue Creating Goals and Projections
- Don't Get Stagnant
- Find a Community
- Thank your Clients/Follow Up
- Celebrate All Wins

Thank You, Thank You, Thank You

I hope all this information finds you well and helps you create your dream business. It is completely up to you to get moving and make this happen! With just $2500, you can start and grow an amazing Home Staging business and thrive for years. It just takes drive, determination, a little creativity, and a love and passion for design. I am humbled you took the time to read this book. I wish you the best of luck in your future endeavors. Happy business creating!!!

-Amy